Tro

This book is published with the aid of the **Bookmarks Publishing Co-operative**. Many socialists have a few savings put aside, probably in a bank or savings bank. While it's there, this money is being loaned out by the bank to some business or other to further the capitalist search for profit. We believe it is better loaned to a socialist venture to further the struggle for socialism. That's how the co-operative works: in return for a loan, repayable at a month's notice, members receive free copies of books published by Bookmarks, plus other advantages. The co-operative has more than 200 members at the time this book is published, from as far apart as London and Australia, Canada and Norway.

Like to know more? Write to the **Bookmarks Publishing Co-operative**, 265 Seven Sisters Road, London N4 2DE, England.

Trotsky's Marxism

Duncan Hallas

Bookmarks
London, Chicago and Melbourne

TROTSKY'S MARXISM
by Duncan Hallas

First published 1979
Published by Bookmarks November 1984,
reprinted December 1987.
Bookmarks, 265 Seven Sisters Road, Finsbury Park,
London N4 2DE, England
Bookmarks, PO Box 16085, Chicago, IL 60616, USA.
Bookmarks, GPO Box 1473N, Melbourne 3001, Australia.
Copyright © Bookmarks and Duncan Hallas.

ISBN 0 906224 15 2

Printed by Cox and Wyman Ltd, Reading, England.
Cover drawing by Tim Saunders.

BOOKMARKS is linked to an international grouping of
socialist organisations:

AUSTRALIA: **International Socialists**, GPO Box
    1473N, Melbourne 3001.
BELGIUM: **Socialisme International**, 9 rue Marexhe,
    4400 Herstal, Liege.
BRITAIN: **Socialist Workers Party**, PO Box 82,
    London E3.
CANADA: **International Socialists**, PO Box 339, Station
    E, Toronto, Ontario.
DENMARK: **Internationale Socialister**, Morten
    Borupsgade 18, kld, 8000 Arhus C.
FRANCE: **Socialisme International** (correspondence to
    Yves Coleman, BP 407, Paris Cedex 05).
IRELAND: **Socialist Workers Movement**, PO Box
    1648, Dublin 8.
NORWAY: **Internasjonale Sosialister**, Postboks 5370
    Majorstua, 0304 Oslo 3.
UNITED STATES: **International Socialist Organization**,
    PO Box 16085, Chicago, Illinois 60616.
WEST GERMANY: **Sozialistische Arbeiter Gruppe**,
    Wolfgangstrasse 81, D–6000 Frankfurt 1.

Contents

Acknowledgements

This little work owes its existence to the encouragement, advice and practical help of Tony Cliff.

Insofar as its treatment of Trotsky's thought is in any way unusual, it is very heavily dependent on Cliff's own appreciation and critique from 1947 onwards. Of course, Cliff is not responsible for every emphasis I have made.

Three other specific acknowledgements must be made. To Nigel Harris, whose writings and conversation have considerably modified my own first assessment of Trotsky; to John Molyneux, whose *Marxism and the Party* has influenced me more than may appear from a superficial view of our respective writings on the subject; and to Chanie Rosenberg who converted my handscript into type in the odd intervals of a very active political life and without whose efforts it would never have seen the light of day.

Duncan Hallas
July 1979

Duncan Hallas is a leading member of the Socialist Workers Party. He writes regularly for the party's monthly *Socialist Worker Review*. His other publications include *The Labour Party: Myth and Reality* (1981), *Days of Hope: The General Strike of 1926* (1981, with Chris Harman) and *The Comintern* (1984).

Introduction

Leon Trotsky was born in 1879 and grew to manhood and to consciousness in a world that has passed away, the world of the social-democratic marxism of the Second International.

In any generation there are many possible mental worlds, rooted in the widely differing circumstances, social organisation and ideologies that co-exist at any one time. That of social democracy was the most advanced, the closest approximation to a scientific, materialist world outlook that then existed.

For Lev Davidovitch Bronstein (the name of Trotsky was borrowed from a jailer), son of a Ukrainian Jewish peasant family, to attain that outlook was remarkable enough. The older Bronstein was a well-to-do peasant, a kulak - otherwise Trotsky would have received very little formal education - and he was a Jew in a country where anti-Semitism was officially encouraged and actual pogroms not rare. At any rate, the young Trotsky became, after an initial period of romantic revolutionism, a marxist. And very soon, under the condition of Tsarist autocracy, a professional revolutionary and a political prisoner. First arrested at the age of 19, he was sentenced to four years' deportation to Siberia after spending 18 months in jail. He escaped in 1902 and, from then until his death, revolution was his profession.

This small book is concerned with ideas rather than events. Least of all is it an attempt at a biography. Isaac Deutscher's three volumes, whatever view is taken of the author's political conclusions, will remain the authoritative biographical study for a very long time.

Yet any attempt to present a summary of Trotsky's ideas

runs into an immediate difficulty. Much more than most of the great marxist thinkers (Lenin is an outstanding exception), Trotsky was concerned throughout his life with the immediate problems facing revolutionaries in the workers' movement. Nearly everything he said or wrote relates to some immediate issue, to some current struggle. The contrast with what has come to be called 'Western marxism' could hardly be more marked. A sympathetic chronicler of this latter trend has written: 'The first and most fundamental of its characteristics has been the structural divorce of this marxism from political practice.'[1] That is the last thing that could ever be said of Trotsky's marxism.

Therefore it is necessary to present, in however sketchy and inadequate a fashion, some elements of the background against which Trotsky formed his ideas.

Russia was backward, Europe advanced. That was the basic idea of all Russian marxists (and not of marxists alone, of course). Europe was advanced because its industrialisation was well developed *and* because social democracy, in the form of sizeable workers' parties professing allegiance to the marxist programme, was growing fast. For Russians (and to some extent generally) the parties of the German speaking countries were the most important. The social-democratic parties of the German and Austrian Empires were expanding workers' parties which had adopted fully marxist programmes (the German Erfurt programme of 1891, the Austrian Heinfeld programme of 1888). Their influence on Russian marxists was immense. The fact that Poland, whose working class was already stirring, was partitioned between the empires of the Tsar and the two Kaisers strengthened the connection. Rosa Luxemburg, it will be recalled, was born in Russian-occupied Poland, but became prominent in the German movement. There was nothing out of the way in this. Social democrats then regarded 'national' boundaries as secondary.

In terms of ideas, this growing movement (illegal in Germany between 1878 and 1890, but polling one and a half million votes on a restricted suffrage in the latter year) was sustained by the synthesis of early marxism and late nineteenth century developments that had been achieved by Friedrich Engels. His *Anti-Dühring* (1878), an attempt at an overall, scientifically grounded world view, was the basis for the popularisations (or vulgarisations) of Karl Kautsky, the 'pope of marxism', and of the more profound expositions of the Russian G.V. Plekhanov.

In this exciting intellectual/practical world - for Engels and his disciples and imitators had established a link between theory and practice in the workers' party - the young Trotsky grew intellectually and soon became something more than a disciple of his elders. His respect for Engels was immense.

Yet he was, within a few years of his first assimilation of the marxist world outlook, to challenge the then marxist orthodoxy on the question of the backward countries. But first he was to meet the emigre leaders of Russian marxism and to play a prominent role in the 1903 congress of the Russian Social Democratic Labour Party - the real founding conference.

Trotsky escaped from Verkholensk in Siberia, hidden under a load of hay, in the summer of 1902. By October he had arrived at the directing centre of Russian social democracy, then situated near Kings Cross station in London. Lenin, Krupskaya, Martov and Vera Zasulich all lived in the area and from here *Iskra*, the organ of the advocates of a centralised, disciplined party, was produced and dispatched to the underground in Russia. Trotsky was soon involved in the disputes within the *Iskra* team - Lenin wished to add him to the editorial board, Plekhanov resolutely opposed the idea - and so came to know at close quarters the future leaders of Menshevism, Plekhanov and Martov, as well as Lenin. For the split in the *Iskra* group was already gestating.

It came into the open at the congress in the summer of 1903. The *Iskra*-ists stood together in resisting the demands of the Jewish socialist organisation, the Bund, for autonomy so far as work amongst Jewish people was concerned, and in resisting the reformist tendency of the Economists. Then came the split in the *Iskra* group itself into the Bolshevik majority and the Menshevik minority.

It was not clear cut at first - the issues themselves were not yet clear. Plekhanov sided with Lenin initially, Trotsky supported the Menshevik leader Martov.

Two years later Trotsky was back in Russia. The revolution of 1905 was under way. In the course of it Trotsky rose to his full height. Still only 26 years old, he became the most prominent single revolutionary leader and an internationally known figure. He emerged from the background of small group and emigre politics transformed into a magnificent orator and mass leader. As President of the Petrograd Soviet he was able to exert a considerable degree of tactical leadership and demonstrated that sure touch and iron nerve which was to characterise him in the greater upheavals of 1917.

The revolution was crushed. The Tsarist army was shaken but not broken. Out of the experience - the 'dress rehearsal' Lenin called it - the divergent tendencies in social democracy moved further apart. Trotsky, still nominally a Menshevik, developed his own unique synthesis, the theory of Permanent Revolution.

The next decade was spent in the small emigre circles again and in futile attempts to unite what were by now incompatible tendencies. Then came the war, anti-war activity and, in February 1917, the overthrow of the Tsar. Trotsky joined the Bolshevik party, by now a real mass workers' party, in July and such was his force of personality, talent and reputation that within a few weeks he stood second only to Lenin in the eyes of the mass of its supporters. He was entrusted with the actual organisation of the October rising and, at the age of 38, became one of the two or three most important figures in party and state, and, a little later, also one of the most significant leaders of the *world* communist movement, the Communist International. He was the main creator and director of the Red Army and influential in every field of policy.

4

From these heights Trotsky was destined to be cast down. The fall was not simply a personal tragedy. Trotsky rose as the revolution rose and fell as the revolution declined. His personal history is fused with the history of the Russian revolution and international socialism. From 1923 he led the opposition to the growing reaction in Russia - to Stalinism. Expelled from the party in 1927 and from the USSR in 1929 his last eleven years were spent in an heroic struggle against impossible odds to keep alive the authentic communist tradition and embody it in a revolutionary organisation. Vilified and isolated, he was finally murdered on Stalin's orders in 1940. He left behind a fragile international organisation and a body of writings that is one of the richest sources of applied marxism in existence.

This book concentrates on four themes. They do not exhaust Trotsky's contribution to marxist thought, not by any means, for he was an exceptionally prolific writer with unusually wide interests.

Nevertheless, his life's work was centrally concerned with these four questions and the bulk of his voluminous writings relate to them in one way or another.

They are, first, the theory of 'Permanent Revolution', its relevance to the Russian revolutions of the twentieth century and to subsequent developments in the colonial and semi-colonial countries - what is today called the 'Third World'.

Second, the outcome of the Russian October revolution and the whole question of Stalinism. Trotsky made the first sustained attempt at an historical materialist analysis of Stalinism and his analysis, whatever criticism may have to be made of it, has been the starting point for all subsequent serious analysis from a marxist point of view.

Third, the strategy and tactics of mass revolutionary parties in a wide variety of situations, a field in which Trotsky's contribution was not inferior to that of Marx and Lenin.

Fourth, the problem of the relationship between party and class and the historical development which reduced the revolutionary movement to a fringe status with respect to the mass workers' organisations.

Isaac Deutscher described Trotsky, in his last years, as 'the residuary legatee of classical marxism'. He was that, and more besides. It is this which gives his thought its enormous contemporary relevance.

1. Permanent Revolution

During the last third of the eighteenth century the industrial revolution, the most profound change in the whole history of the human race since the development of agriculture in the remote past, gained an irresistible momentum in one small corner of the world, in Britain. But the British capitalists soon had imitators in those other countries where a bourgeoisie had gained power or come near to gaining power.

By the beginning of the present century industrial capitalism completely dominated the world. The colonial empires of Britain, France, Germany, Russia, the USA, Belgium, the Netherlands, Italy and Japan covered by far the greater part of the world's land surface. Those essentially pre-capitalist societies that still preserved a nominal independence (China, Iran, the Turkish Empire, Ethiopia, etc.) were, in fact, dominated by one or other of the great imperialist powers or informally partitioned between them - the term 'spheres of influence' expresses it exactly. Such token 'independence' as remained was due solely to the rivalries of competing imperialisms (Britain versus Russia in Iran; Britain versus France in Thailand; Britain versus Germany - with Russia as an also-ran - in Turkey; Britain, the USA, Germany, Russia, France, Japan and various minor contenders, all against each other, in China).

Yet the countries conquered or dominated by the industrial capitalist powers were *not*, generally speaking, transformed into replicas of the various 'mother countries'. On the contrary, they remained essentially pre-industrial societies. Their social and economic development was profoundly influenced - profoundly distorted - by conquest or dominance, but they were not, typically, transformed into the new type of society.

Marx's famous description of the ruin of the Indian textile industry (which had been based on high quality products made by independent artisans) by cheap Lancashire machine-made cotton piece goods still stands as a good rough outline of the initial impact of Western capitalism on what is now called the 'Third World': impoverishment and social retrogression.

This process of 'combined and uneven development', to use Trotsky's expression, led to a situation (still with us in all essentials) in which the greater part of the world's population had not only not advanced socially and economically, but had been thrown backwards. What then, was (and, indeed, is) the way forward for the mass of the people in these countries?

Trotsky, as a young man of 26, made a profoundly original contribution to the solution of this problem. It was a solution rooted both in the realities of the uneven development of capitalism on a world scale, and in the marxist analysis of the true significance of industrial development - the creation, at one and the same time, of the material basis for an advanced classless society and of an exploited class, the proletariat, which is capable of raising itself to the level of a ruling class and, through its rule, of abolishing classes, the class struggle, and all forms of alienation and oppression.

Trotsky, naturally, developed his ideas in relation to Russia in the first instance. It is therefore necessary to look at the ideological background to the disputes amongst Russian revolutionaries in the late nineteenth and early twentieth centuries in order to understand the full import of his contribution. But not only Russian revolutionaries. There was, after all, a real international movement at that time.

Once Europe is reorganised, and North America, that will furnish such colossal power and such an example that the semi-civilised countries will follow in their wake of their own accord. Economic needs alone will be responsible for this. But as to what social and political phases these countries will then have to pass through before they likewise arrive at socialist organisation, we today can only advance rather idle hypotheses, I think. One thing alone is certain; the victorious proletariat can force no blessings of any kind on any foreign nation without undermining its own victory by so doing.[1]

So Engels wrote to Kautsky in 1882. He was not thinking of Russia. The countries mentioned in this letter are India, Algeria, Egypt and the 'Dutch, Portuguese and Spanish possessions'. Nevertheless, his general approach is representative of the thinking of what was to become the Second International (from 1889 onwards). The course of political development would follow the course of economic development. The revolutionary socialist movement that would destroy capitalism and lead ultimately to the dissolution of the proletariat and all classes (after a period of proletarian dictatorship) into the classless society of the future would develop where capitalism and its inseparable concomitant the proletariat had first developed.

Russian marxists, of which the pioneer 'Emancipation of Labour' group was founded the year after Engels's letter was written, had to place Russia in this historical scheme.

Plekhanov, the leading light of the group, had no doubts. The Russian Empire, he argued in the eighties and nineties, was an essentially pre-capitalist society and therefore was destined to go through the process of capitalist development before the question of socialism could be addressed. He firmly rejected the idea, with which Marx himself had once toyed, that Russia might, depending on developments in Europe, avoid the capitalist stage of development altogether and achieve a transition to socialism on the basis of a peasant movement overthrowing the autocracy and seeking to preserve the elements of traditional communal ownership of land (the Mir) which still existed in the 1880s.

9

Plekhanov's views, developed in polemics with the 'peasant road to socialism' school (the Narodniks), became the starting point for all subsequent Russian marxism. That capitalism was in fact developing in Russia, that the Mir was doomed, that a special 'Russian road to socialism' was a reactionary illusion - these ideas were basic for the next generation of Russian marxists, for Lenin and, a few years later, for Trotsky and for all their associates. The first three volumes of Lenin's *Collected Works* consist very largely of criticism of the Narodniks and demonstrations of the inevitability - and progressive character - of capitalism in Russia. The *Iskra* group, founded in 1900 to create a unified national organisation out of the scattered social-democratic groups and circles, based itself firmly on the view that the industrial working class was the basis for that organisation.

Three questions arose: first, what was the *relationship* between the political roles of the working class (still a small minority), the bourgeoisie and the peasantry (the great majority); hence, what was the *class character* of the coming revolution in Russia; finally, what was the relationship between the revolution and the working class movements of the advanced countries of the West?

The different answers given to these questions was one of the two main issues (the other being the nature of the revolutionary party) that defined what were to become fundamentally divergent tendencies. To understand Trotsky's theory of Permanent Revolution it is necessary to look briefly at these answers, as they appeared in developed form after the 1905 revolution.

Menshevism

The Menshevik view can be summarised in this way: the state of the development of the productive forces (that is, Russia's general economic backwardness combined with a small but significant and growing modern industry) defines what is possible - a *bourgeois* revolution, like that of 1789-94 in France. Therefore the bourgeoisie must come to power, establish a bourgeois-democratic republic which will sweep away the remnants of pre-capitalist social relations and open the road to a rapid growth of the productive forces (and so of the proletariat) on a *capitalist* basis. The struggle for the socialist revolution will thus, eventually, come onto the agenda.

The political role of the working class is, therefore, to push the bourgeoisie forward against Tsarism. It must preserve its political independence - meaning, centrally, that social democrats cannot enter into a revolutionary government alongside non-proletarian forces.

As to the peasantry, it cannot play an *independent* political role. It can play a secondary revolutionary role in support of the essentially urban bourgeois revolution and, after that revolution, will undergo more or less rapid economic differentiation into a layer of capitalist farmers (which will be conservative), a layer of small-holders and a layer of landless agricultural proletarians.

There is no organic connection between the Russian bourgeois revolution and the European workers' movement, although the Russian revolution (if it occurs before the socialist revolution in the West) will invigorate the Western social democracies.

Actually, Menshevism was a rather variegated tendency. Different Mensheviks put different emphases on the several parts of this scheme (which, as presented, is essentially Plekhanov's) but all accepted its general contours.

The 1905 revolution showed up its fundamental flaws. The bourgeoisie would not play the part allocated to it. Of course, Plekhanov, a profound student of the great French Revolution, never expected the Russian bourgeoisie to lead a ruthless struggle against Tsarism without enormous pressure from below. Just as the Jacobin dictatorship of 1793-94, the decisive culmination of the French Revolution, had come to power under the violent pressure of the *sans-culottes*, the plebeian

11

masses of Paris, so in Russia the working class could be the real driving force, *compelling* the bourgeoisie's political representatives (or a section of them) to take power. But 1905 and its aftermath demonstrated that there was no 'Robespierrist' tendency in the Russian bourgeoisie. Faced with revolutionary upsurge it rallied to the Tsar.

Already in 1898 the Manifesto drawn up for the abortive First Congress of Russian Social Democrats had declared:

> The farther east one goes in Europe, the more the bourgeoisie becomes in the political respect weaker, more cowardly, and meaner, and the larger are the cultural and political tasks which fall to the share of the proletariat.[2]

It was not a matter of geography but of history. The development of industrial capitalism and of the modern proletariat had made the bourgeoisie everywhere, even in countries where industrialisation was embryonic, a conservative class. Indeed, the failure of the revolution in Germany in 1848-49 had demonstrated this much earlier.

Bolshevism

The Bolsheviks' view started from the same premises as the Mensheviks'. The coming revolution would be, and could only be, a *bourgeois* revolution in terms of its class nature. It went on to reject outright any reliance on pressurising the bourgeoisie, and to propose an alternative.

> The transformation of the economic and political situation in Russia along bourgeois-democratic lines is inevitable and inescapable,

wrote Lenin in his famous pamphlet *Two Tactics of Social Democracy in the Democratic Revolution* (July 1905).

> No power on earth can prevent such a transformation, but the combined action of the existing forces which are

12

effecting it may result in either of two things, may bring about either of two forms of that transformation. Either 1) matters will end in 'the revolution's decisive victory over Tsarism' or 2) the forces will be inadequate for a decisive victory, and matters will end in a deal with the most 'inconsistent' and most 'self-seeking' elements of the bourgeoisie... We must be perfectly certain in our own minds as to what real social forces are opposed to Tsarism... and are capable of gaining a 'decisive victory' over it. The big bourgeoisie... cannot be such a force. We see that they do not even want a decisive victory. We know that owing to their class position they are incapable of waging a decisive struggle against Tsarism; they are too heavily fettered by private property, by capital and land to enter into a decisive struggle. They stand in too great a need of Tsarism, with its bureaucratic, police and military forces to use against the proletariat and peasantry to want it to be destroyed. No, the only force capable of gaining 'a decisive victory over Tsarism' is the *people*, i.e., the proletariat and the peasantry... 'The revolution's decisive victory over Tsarism' means the establishment of the *revolutionary-democratic dictatorship of the proletariat and the peasantry*...

It can only be a dictatorship, for realisation of the changes urgently and absolutely indispensible to the proletariat and the peasantry will evoke desperate resistance from the landlords, the big bourgeoisie and Tsarism... But of course it will be a democratic, not a socialist dictatorship... At best, it may bring about a radical redistribution of landed property in favour of the peasantry, establish consistent and full democracy, including the formation of a republic, eradicate all the oppressive features of Asiatic bondage, not only in rural but also in factory life, lay the foundations for a thorough improvement in the conditions of the workers and for a rise in their standard of living, and - last but not least - carry the

13

revolutionary conflagration into Europe. Such a victory will not yet by any means transform our bourgeois revolution into a socialist revolution . . . [3]

The Menshevik line was not simply a mistake, Lenin argued, it was the expression of an unwillingness to carry through the revolution. Menshevik determination to cling to the bourgeois liberals must lead to paralysis. The peasantry, on the other hand, had a genuine interest in the destruction of Tsarism and the remnants of feudalism on the land. Therefore the 'democratic dictatorship' - a provisional revolutionary government, with representatives of the peasantry included alongside social democrats - was the appropriate 'Jacobin' regime that would crush the reaction and establish 'a democratic republic (with complete equality and self-determination for all nations), confiscation of the landed estates, and an eight hour working day'.[4]

Trotsky's Solution
Trotsky rejected the reliance on a 'revolutionary bourgeoisie' as firmly as Lenin. He ridiculed the Menshevik scheme as

an extra-historical category created by journalistic analogy and deduction . . . because, in France, the Revolution was carried through to the end by democratic revolutionaries - the Jacobins - therefore the Russian revolution can transfer power only into the hands of a revolutionary bourgois democracy. Having thus erected an unshakeable algebraic formula of revolution, the Mensheviks then try to insert into it arithmetical values which do not in fact exist.[5]

In every other respect Trotsky's theory of Permanent Revolution, which owed a good deal to the Russo-German marxist Parvus, differed from the Bolshevik position.

14

First, and crucially, it ruled out the possibility that the peasantry could play an *independent* political role:

> the peasantry cannot play a leading revolutionary role. History cannot entrust the muzhik with the task of liberating a bourgeois nation from its bonds. Because of its dispersion, political backwardness, and especially of its deep inner contradictions which cannot be resolved within the framework of a capitalist system, the peasantry can only deal the old order some powerful blows from the rear, by spontaneous risings in the countryside, on the one hand, and by creating discontent within the army on the other.[6]

This was identical with the Menshevik line and followed Marx's own assessment of the French peasantry as a class.

Because 'the town leads in modern society', only an urban class can play a *leading* role and because the bourgeoisie is not revolutionary (and the urban petty-bourgeoisie in any case is incapable of playing the part of *sans-culottes*),

> the conclusion remains that only the proletariat in its class struggle, placing the peasant masses under its revolutionary leadership, can 'carry the revolution to the end'.[7]

This *must* lead to a *workers'* government, Lenin's 'democratic dictatorship' is simply an illusion:

> *The political domination of the proletariat is incompatible with its economic enslavement. No matter under what political flag the proletariat has come to power, it is obliged to take the path of socialist policy.* It would be the greatest utopianism to think that the proletariat, having been raised to political domination by the internal mechanism of a bourgeois revolution can, even if it so desires, limit its mission to the creation of republican-democratic conditions for the social domination of the bourgeoisie.[8]

But this leads to an immediate contradiction. The common

starting point of all Russian marxists was precisely that Russia lacked both the material and human basis for socialism - a highly developed industry and a modern proletariat making up a large fraction of the population and having acquired organisation and consciousness as a class 'for itself', as Marx had put it. Lenin had denounced forcefully (in *Two Tactics*):

> The absurd and semi-anarchist idea of giving immediate effect to the maximum programme and the conquest of power for a socialist revolution. The degree of economic development (an objective condition), and the development of class consciousness and organisation of the broad masses of the proletariat (a subjective condition inseparably bound up with the objective condition) make the immediate and complete emancipation of the working class impossible. Only the most ignorant people can close their eyes to the bourgeois nature of the democratic revolution which is now taking place [in 1905].[9]

From a marxist standpoint, Lenin's argument is incontestible so long as matters stand on the ground of Russia alone. It is perhaps necessary, in view of subsequent developments, to stress this elementary point. Socialism, for Marx and for all those who regarded themselves as his followers at that time, is the self-emancipation of the working class. It therefore presupposes both large-scale modern industry and a class-conscious proletariat capable of self-emancipation.

Trotsky was nevertheless convinced that only the working class was capable of playing the leading role in the Russian revolution and, if it did so, could not fail to take power into its own hands. What then?

> The revolutionary authorities will be confronted with the objective problems of socialism, but the solution of these problems will, at a certain stage, be prevented by the country's economic backwardness. *There is no way out from this contradiction within the framework of a national*

16

revolution. The workers' government will from the start be faced with the task of uniting its forces with those of the socialist proletariat of Western Europe. Only in this way will its temporary revolutionary hegemony become the prologue to a socialist dictatorship. Thus, permanent revolution will become, for the Russian proletariat, a matter of class self-preservation.[10]

Engel's original hypothesis is turned upside down. The *uneven* development of capitalism leads to a *combined* development in which backward Russia becomes, temporarily, the vanguard of an international socialist revolution.

The theory of Permanent Revolution remained central to Trotsky's marxism to the end of his life. In only one important respect did his post-1917 ideas on the question differ from those outlined. The pre-1917 version depended heavily on spontaneous working class action. As we shall see, Trotsky was in this period a strong opponent of 'Bolshevik centralism' and rejected in practice the conception of the leading role of the party. In 1917 he reversed his position on this issue. His subsequent applications of the theory of Permanent Revolution were structured around the role of the revolutionary workers' party.

The Outcome
All theory, at least all theory which has any pretensions to be scientific, finds its ultimate test in practice. 'The proof of the pudding', as the Lancashire saying goes, 'is in the eating'. But the *decisive* practical test may be long delayed, delayed long after the deaths of the theorist and his or her supporters and opponents.

Unlike the physical sciences - where it is always possible *in principle* to set up experimental tests (even though the technical means to carry them through may not be immediately available) - marxism as the science of social development (and, indeed, its bourgeois rivals, the pseudo-sciences of economics,

17

sociology and so on) cannot be tested according to some arbitrary time scale but only in the course of historical development and, even then, only provisionally.

The reason is simple enough, although the consequences are immensely complicated. 'Men make their own history', Marx said, 'although they do not do so under conditions of their own choosing'. The 'voluntary' acts of millions and tens of millions of people who are, of course, themselves historically conditioned, pressing against constraints imposed by the whole course of previous historical development (of which the millions are, typically, unaware) produces effects more complex than the most far-sighted theorist can foresee. The degree of *on s'engage, et puis . . . on voit* (get stuck in, and then we'll see) which was Napoleon's aphoristic description of his military science, must always be considerable for revolutionaries engaged in a conscious attempt to shape the course of events.

The Russian revolutionaries of the early twentieth century were more fortunate than most. For them the decisive test came very quickly. 1917 saw the Mensheviks, the opponents *in principle* of participation in a non-proletarian government, join a government of opponents of socialism in order to prosecute an imperialist war and hold back the tide of revolution. It verified *in practice* Lenin's 1905 prediction that they were the 'Gironde' of the Russian revolution.

It saw the Bolsheviks, the advocates of the democratic dictatorship and a coalition Provisional Revolutionary Government, after an initial period of 'critical support' for what Lenin, on his return to Russia, called 'a government of capitalists', turn decisively towards the seizure of power by the *working class* under the impact of Lenin's *April Theses* and the pressure of the revolutionary workers in their ranks.

It saw Trotsky brilliantly vindicated when Lenin, in effect although not in words, adopted the Permanent Revolution perspective and abandoned the democratic dictatorship without ceremony.

It also saw Trotsky in practice isolated and impotent to

18

affect the course of events in the great revolutionary crisis of 1917 until, in July, he led his smallish and largely intellectual following into the mass Bolshevik party. It therefore saw Lenin's long, hard struggle (which Trotsky had denounced for more than a decade as 'sectarian') for a *workers*' party, free from the ideological influence of petty-bourgeois 'marxists' (so far as such independence can be achieved by organisational means) no less brilliantly vindicated.[11]

Trotsky had been proved right on the central strategic issue of the Russian revolution. But, as Cliff justly remarks, he was 'a brilliant general without an army to speak of'.[12] Trotsky never subsequently forgot that fact. He was later to write that his breach with Lenin, on the question of the need for a disciplined workers' party in 1903-04, was 'the greatest mistake of my life'.

The October revolution put the Russian working class in power. It did so in the context of a rising tide of revolutionary revolt against the old regimes in central and, to a lesser degree, western Europe.

Trotsky's perspective, and Lenin's after April 1917, depended crucially on the success of the *proletarian* revolution in at least 'one or two' (as Lenin, always cautious, put it), advanced countries.

In the event, the power of the established social-democratic parties (which proved in practice, from August 1914 on to have become conservative and nationalistic) and the vacillations and evasions of the leaders of the mass 'centrist' breakaways from them between 1916 and 1921, aborted the revolutionary movements in Germany, Austria, Hungary, Italy and elsewhere before the proletarian revolution could be achieved or, where temporarily achieved, consolidated.

Trotsky's analysis of the consequences of these facts will be examined later. But first it will be useful to look at the second Chinese Revolution (of 1925-27), and its outcome in terms of Trotsky's theory.

The Chinese Revolution 1925-27

The Chinese Communist Party (CCP) was founded in July 1921 against a background of rising anti-imperialist feelings and working class militancy in the coastal cities where the newly created but sizeable industrial working class was struggling to organise itself.

Tiny and composed at first entirely of intellectuals, the CCP was able in a few years to become the effective leadership of the newly born labour movement.

China was then a semi-colony, partitioned informally between British, French, United States and Japanese imperialisms. German and Russian imperialisms had been eliminated by war and revolution before 1919.

Each imperialist power maintained its own 'sphere of influence' and supported 'its own' regional baron, war-lord or 'national' government. Thus the British, then the dominant imperialist power, gave arms, money and 'advisers' to Wu P'ei-fu, the dominant warlord in central China, who controlled the districts along the Yangtse River. The Japanese rendered the same services to Chang Tso-lin, war-lord of Manchuria. Lesser military gangsters, each one shiftingly attached to one or other imperialist power, controlled most of the rest of the country.

The exception, a very partial exception, was Canton and its hinterland. Here Sun Yat-sen, the father of Chinese nationalism, had established some sort of a base on a programme of national independence, modernisation and social reforms with a vague 'leftist' veneer. Sun's party, the Kuomintang (KMT), a fairly formless and ineffective body before 1922, depended on the toleration of the local 'progressive' warlord.

However, after preliminary moves from 1922 onwards, the KMT leaders made an agreement with the government of the USSR which in 1924 sent political and military advisers to Canton and began to supply arms. The KMT became a centralised party with a relatively efficient army. Moreover from late

1922 the members of the CCP were sent into the KMT 'as individuals'. Three of them even sat on the KMT Executive. This policy, which had met with some resistance in the CCP, was imposed by the Executive of the Communist International. The CCP was, in effect, tied to the KMT.

Then, in the early summer of 1925 a mass strike movement - partly economic in origin but rapidly politicised in the repression attempted by foreign troops and police - broke out in Shanghai and spread to the major cities of central and south China, including Canton and Hong Kong. With many ups and downs an enormous mass movement of revolt existed in the cities until early 1927. At various times a situation of dual power existed, with CCP-led strike committees constituting 'Government Number Two'. And in those same years peasant revolts broke out in a number of important provinces. The war-lord regimes were shaken to their foundations. The KMT sought to ride the storm with the help of the CCP, and then to exploit it to conquer national power without social change. Early in 1926 the KMT was admitted to the Communist International as a sympathising party!

Trotsky, although still a member of the political bureau of the Russian party, was effectively excluded from direct influence on policy by 1925. According to Deutscher,[13] he called for the withdrawal of the CCP from the KMT in April 1926. His first substantial written criticism dates from September.

> The revolutionary struggle in China has, since 1925, entered a new phase, which is characterised above all by the active intervention of broad layers of the proletariat. At the same time, the commercial bourgeoisie and the elements of the intelligentsia linked with it, are breaking off to the right, assuming a hostile attitude towards strikes, communists and the USSR. It is quite clear that in the light of these fundamental facts the question of revising relations between the Communist Party and the Kuomintang must necessarily be raised...

21

The leftward movement of the masses of Chinese workers is as certain a fact as the rightward movement of the Chinese bourgeoisie. Insofar as the Kuomintang has been based on the political and organisational union of the workers and the bourgeoisie, it must now be torn apart by the centrifugal tendencies of the class struggle...

The participation of the CCP in the Kuomintang was perfectly correct in the period in which the CCP was a propaganda society which was only preparing itself for future *independent* political activity but which, at the same time, sought to take part in the ongoing national liberation struggle...But the fact of the Chinese proletariat's mighty awakening, its desire for struggle and for independent class organisation, is absolutely undeniable...Its [the CCP's] immediate political task must now be to fight for direct independent leadership of the awakened working class - not of course to remove the working class from the national-revolutionary struggle, but to assure it the role of not only the most resolute fighter, but also of political leader with hegemony in the struggle of the Chinese masses...

To think that the petty-bourgeoisie can be won over by clever manoeuvres or good advice within the Kuomintang is hopeless utopianism. The Communist Party will be more able to exert direct and indirect influence upon the petty-bourgeoisie of town and country the stronger the party is in itself, that is, the more the party has won over the Chinese working class. But that is possible only on the basis of an independent class party and class policy.[14]

This was totally unacceptable to Stalin and his associates. Their policy was to cling to the KMT and to force the CCP to subordinate itself, no matter what. In this way they hoped a reliable ally of the USSR could be kept going in South China and, perhaps, later could take power nationally.

This policy was justified theoretically by reviving the 'democratic dictatorship' thesis. The Chinese revolution was a bourgeois revolution and therefore, the argument went, a democratic dictatorship of the proletariat and peasantry should be the aim. In order to preserve the worker-peasant bloc the movement must confine itself to 'democratic' demands. The socialist revolution was not on the agenda. The difficulty presented by the fact that the KMT was manifestly *not* a peasant party was met by the argument that actually it was a multiclass party, a 'bloc of four classes' (bourgeoisie, urban petty bourgeoisie, workers and peasants).

> What does this mean anyway - bloc of four classes? Have you ever encountered this expression in Marxist literature before? If the bourgeoisie leads the oppressed masses of the people under the bourgeois banner and takes hold of state power through its leadership, then this is no bloc but the political exploitation of the oppressed masses by the bourgeoisie.[15]

The real point is that the bourgeoisie would capitulate to the imperialists. Therefore the KMT would inevitably play a counter-revolutionary role.

> The Chinese bourgeoisie is sufficiently realistic and acquainted intimately enough with the nature of world imperialism to understand that a really serious struggle against the latter requires such an upheaval of the revolutionary masses as would primarily become a menace to the bourgeoisie itself ... And if we taught the workers of Russia from the very beginning not to believe in the readiness of liberalism and the ability of petty-bourgeois democracy to crush Tsarism and to destroy feudalism, we should no less energetically imbue the Chinese workers from the outset with the same spirit of distrust. The new and absolutely false theory promulgated by Stalin-Bukharin about the 'immanent' revolutionary spirit of

23

the colonial bourgeoisie is, in substance, a translation of Menshevism into the language of Chinese politics.[16]

The outcome is well known. Chiang Kai-shek, military chief of the KMT, mounted his first coup against the left in Canton in March 1926. The CCP, under Russian pressure, submitted. When Chiang's army launched the 'Northern Expedition' a wave of working class and peasant revolt destroyed the war-lord forces, but the CCP, faithful to the 'bloc', did its best to prevent 'excesses'. Before Chiang entered Shanghai in March 1927, the war-lord forces were defeated by two general strikes and an insurrection led by the CCP. Chiang ordered the workers to be disarmed. The CCP refused to resist. Then, in April, they were massacred and the labour movement was beheaded. There followed a split in the KMT. The civilian leaders, fearing (correctly) that Chiang was out to become military dictator, set up their government in Wuhan (Hankow).

The CCP was now required by the Comintern to support this 'left' KMT regime, and supplied its ministers of labour and agriculture. Its leader, Wang Ching-wei, used them to serve his turn and then, after a few months, carried out his own coup. Subsequently he even headed the puppet government of Japanese-occupied China. The CCP was driven underground and rapidly lost its mass base in the towns. At each crucial confrontation it had used its hard-earned influence to persuade the workers not to resist the KMT.

Then, because a critical stage had been reached in the inner party struggle in Russia, the Stalin-Bukharin ruling group in the Communist Party of the Soviet Union (CPSU) made a 180 degree turn. From repeated capitulations to the KMT, the CCP was forced into an outright putsch. Stalin and Bukharin needed a victory in China in order to fend off the criticisms of the opposition (which they planned to expel) at the fifteenth Congress of the CPSU in December 1927. A new Comintern emissary, Heinz Neumann, was sent to Canton where he attempted to stage a coup d'etat in early December. The CCP still had a serious underground force in the city. Five thousand communists, mostly local workers, took part in the rising. But there had been no political preparation, no agitation, no involvement of the mass of the working class. The communists were isolated. This 'Canton Commune' was crushed in approximately the same time it had taken to crush Blanqui's insurrection in Paris in 1839 - two days - and for the same reasons. It was a putsch undertaken without regard to the level of the class struggle and the consciousness of the working class. The outcome was a massacre even greater than that of Shanghai. The CCP ceased to exist in Canton.

The theory of Permanent Revolution had been strikingly confirmed again - in a negative sense. Imperialist domination of China got a further lease of life.

Suppose, however, the CCP had followed the same course as the Bolsheviks had followed after April 1917. Was a proletarian dictatorship really possible in a country as backward as China was in the nineteen-twenties?

Trotsky was open-minded:

The question of the 'non-capitalistic' path of development of China was posed in a conditional form by Lenin, for whom, as for us, it was and is ABC wisdom that the Chinese revolution, left to its own forces, that is, *without the direct support of the victorious proletariat of the USSR and the working class of all countries*, could end only with the broadest possibilities for capitalist development of the country, with more favourable conditions for the labour movement . . . But first of all, the inevitability of the capitalist path has by no means been proved; and secondly - the argument is incomparably more timely for us - the bourgeois tasks can be solved in various ways.[17]

It will be necessary to return to that last point. In the second half of this century a series of revolutions have occurred, from Angola through to Cuba and Vietnam to Zanzibar (now part of Tanzania), which were certainly not

25

proletarian revolutions and were certainly not bourgeois revolutions in the classic sense.

Trotsky did not foresee such a development, nor did anyone else in his time. The theory of Permanent Revolution, decisively confirmed in the first half of this century, must obviously be reconsidered in the light of these later developments. The question will be taken up in the final chapter below.

2. Stalinism

The dream of and the hope for a classless and truly free society is very old. In Europe it is well documented from the fourteenth century onwards in the fragments that survive of the ideas of many rebels and heretics. 'When Adam delved and Eve span, who was then the gentleman?' went the rhyme popular during the great English peasant revolt of 1381. And, of course, similar sentiments can be identified (however over-laden with ruling class ideology) in early Christianity and early Islam and, in varying degrees, in societies very much older than these.

Marx introduced a fundamentally new idea. It can be summarised as follows: the aspirations of the most advanced thinkers and activists of past (pre-industrial) generations, how-ever admirable and inspiring for the future, were utopian in their own time in the simple sense that they were unrealisable. Class society, exploitation and oppression are inevitable so long as the development of the productive forces and the productivity of labour (related but not identical concepts) are at a comparatively low level. With the growth of industrial capitalism such things are no longer *inevitable*, provided capitalism is overthrown. A classless society, based on (relative) plenty is now possible. Moreover, the instrument for achieving such a society - the industrial proletariat - has been brought into existence by the development of capitalism itself.

These ideas were, of course, the common coin of pre-1914 marxism. All revolutionaries in the marxist tradition took them for granted. But the society that came out of the Russian October revolution was not a free and classless society. Even at an early stage, it deviated a long way from Marx's view of a workers' state (as explained in *The Civil War in France*) or Lenin's development of Marx (as expounded in *State and Revolution*). Later, it grew into a monstrous despotism.

It would be difficult to exaggerate the importance of these facts. The existence, first of one state, and now a whole series of states, claiming to be 'socialist' but which are repulsive caricatures of socialism, must be reckoned as a major factor in the survival of 'Western capitalism'.

Right-wing propagandists argue that Stalinism, or something like it, is the inevitable result of expropriating the capitalist class. Social-democratic propagandists, on the other hand, argue that Stalinism is the inevitable consequence of 'Bolshevik centralism', and that Stalin was 'Lenin's natural heir'.

Trotsky made the first *sustained* attempt at a historical materialist analysis of Stalinism - of the actual outcome of the Russian revolution. Whatever criticisms can be made of it - and some will be made here - it has been the starting point for all subsequent *serious* analysis from a marxist point of view.

What was the social reality of the Russia of 1921, when Lenin was still chairman of the Council of People's Commissars and Trotsky still the People's Commissar for War?

Speaking in support of the New Economic Policy in the USSR in late 1921, Lenin argued that:

> if capitalism gains by it, industrial production will grow, and the proletariat will grow too. The capitalists will gain from our policy and will create an industrial proletariat, which in our country, owing to the war and to the desperate poverty and ruin, has become declassed, i.e., dislodged from its class groove, and has ceased to exist as a proletariat. The proletariat is the class which is engaged in the production of material values in large-scale capitalist industry. Since large-scale capitalist industry has been destroyed, since the factories are at a standstill, the proletariat has disappeared. It has sometimes figured in statistics, but it has not been held together economically.[1]

28

The proletariat 'has ceased to exist as a proletariat'! What then becomes of the proletarian dictatorship, the proletariat as ruling class?

War and civil war wrecked Russian industry - already very weak by Western standards. From the October revolution till March 1918, when the 'monstrous robber treaty' of Brest Litovsk was signed with Germany, revolutionary Russia remained at war with Germany and Austria-Hungary. The following month the first of the 'allied' armies of intervention - the Japanese - landed at Vladivostok and began to push on into Siberia. It was not to withdraw finally until November 1922. In those years detachments of fourteen foreign armies (including those of the United States, Britain and France) invaded the territory of the revolutionary republic. 'White' generals were armed, supplied and supported. At the height of the intervention, in the summer of 1919, the Soviet republic was reduced to a rump state in central European Russia around Moscow with a few outlying bastions precariously held. Even in the following summer, when the 'white' armies had been decisively beaten, one quarter of the entire available grain supply of the Soviet republic had to be sent to the western army group fighting the Polish invaders.

This at a time when the cities were depopulated and starving. More than half the total population of Petrograd (Leningrad) and nearly half that of Mowcow had fled to the countryside. Such industry as could be kept going was devoted almost entirely to war - and this was made possible only by 'cannibalisation', the steady sacrifice of the productive base as a whole in order to keep a fraction of it working. These were the circumstances in which the Russian proletariat, a small minority to start with, disintegrated.

The facts are known well enough and are set out in some detail in, for example, the second volume of E.H. Carr's *The Bolshevik Revolution*.[2] By 1921 total industrial output stood at roughly *one eighth* of the 1913 figure, itself a wretchedly low figure by German, British or US standards.

The revolution survived by means of enormous exertions, directed by a revolutionary dictatorship which far surpassed the Jacobin dictatorship of 1793 in its mobilising capacity. But it survived at the cost of a ruined economy. And it remained isolated. By 1921 the European revolutionary movement was clearly at an ebb.

What concerns us here are the social consequences of these facts. The so-called 'war communism' of 1918-21 had been, in reality, a siege economy of the most brutal and brutalising kind. In essence it consisted of forced requisitioning of grain from the peasantry, the cannibalisation of industry, universal conscription and massive coercion to win the war for survival.

Before the revolution a substantial part of the peasants' grain production had been diverted to the cities (directly or via exports) in the form of rents, interest payments, taxes, compensation payments and so on, to the old ruling classes. Tsarist Russia had been a major grain exporter. Now, with the destruction of the old order, that link was cut. The peasants produced for consumption - or for exchange. But the ruin of industry meant that there was nothing, or nearly nothing, to exchange. Hence forced requisitioning.

The revolution had survived in an overwhelmingly peasant country because of the support - usually passive but sometimes active - of the peasant masses who had gained from it. With the end of the civil war they had no more to gain and the revolts in 1921, in Kronstadt and Tambov, showed that the peasantry and sections of the remnants of the working class were turning against the regime.

The New Economic Policy (NEP) of 1921 onwards recognised this fact above all and introduced a fixed tax (levied in grain, since money had become worthless under war communism) in place of the arbitrary requisitioning of that era. Secondly, it allowed the revival of private trade and private small-scale production (retaining the 'commanding heights' for the state). Thirdly, it opened the gates (pretty unsuccessfully) for foreign capital to exploit 'concessions'. Fourthly, and this was vitally important, the NEP introduced the strict enforcement of the principle of profitability in most of the nationalised industries, along with a strict financial orthodoxy, based on a gold standard, to produce a stable currency and to impose the discipline of the market on public and private enterprises alike.

These measures, introduced between 1921 and 1928, did indeed produce an economic revival. It went slowly at first, and then more quickly, until by 1926-27 the levels of *industrial* output of 1913 were reached and, in a few cases, exceeded. In the case of *disposable* foodstuffs (mainly grain) the growth was much slower. Output grew but the peasantry, no longer exploited as in 1913, consumed much more of their output than before the revolution, so the cities continued to exist on short rations.

Achieved by capitalist or quasi-capitalist measures, this economic recovery had corresponding social consequences.

> And now the cities we ruled over assumed a foreign aspect; we felt ourselves sinking into the mire - paralysed, corrupted ... Money lubricated the entire machine just as under capitalism. A million and a half unemployed received relief - inadequate relief - in the big towns ... Classes were reborn under our very eyes; at the bottom of the scale the unemployed received 24 roubles a month, at the top the engineer (i.e., the technical specialist) receiving 800, and between the two the party functionary with 222 but obtaining a good many things free of charge. There was a growing chasm between the prosperity of the few and the misery of the many.[3]

As a result of the NEP the working class did undergo a numerical revival from the low point of 1921 but it did not revive politically - or not on a scale sufficient to shake the power of the bureaucrat, the 'Nepman' and the kulak. The whip of mass unemployment - much more severe proportionately

in the Russia of the twenties than in the Britain of the thirties -
was a major factor.

A Distorted Workers' State

The disintegration of the working class had reached an
advanced stage when, towards the end of 1920, the so-called
'trade union debate' broke out in the Russian CP.

The issue at stake was, on the surface, whether or not
workers needed trade union organisation to defend themselves
against 'their own' state. At a deeper level the conflict was
about much more fundamental questions.

Did the workers' state of 1918 still exist? Soviet democracy
had, in practice, been destroyed in the civil war. The Communist Party had 'emancipated' itself from the need for majority
working class support. The soviets had become rubber stamps
for party decisions. Moreover, the process of 'militarisation'
and 'commandism' within the Communist Party had grown
apace, and for the same reasons.

Against these developments, the 'Workers' Opposition' in
the party revolted. They called for 'autonomy' for the unions,
denouncing party control and appealing to a tradition of
'workers' control of production' (a party demand in an earlier
period). If adopted, these measures would have meant the end
of the regime - for the bulk of what remained of the working
class was by now decidedly indifferent, if not anti-Bolshevik.
So, too, increasingly, was the mass of the peasantry, which was
the great majority of the population. 'Democracy' under these
conditions could only mean counter-revolution - and a right
wing dictatorship.

The party had been driven to substitute itself for a vanishing
working class and, within the party, the leading bodies had increasingly asserted their authority over a growing but ill-assorted
membership. (The RCP had in round figures 115,000 members
in early 1918, 313,000 by early 1919, 650,000 by the summer
of 1921 - a shrinking minority of them, workers at the bench).

The party had become the trustee for a working class that, temporarily it was hoped, had become incapable of managing its affairs. But the party itself was not immune from the immensely powerful social forces generated by industrial decline, low (and falling) productivity of labour, cultural backwardness and barbarism. Indeed, for the party to act as 'trustee' it was necessary to deprive the mass of its membership of any effective say in the direction of events - for they too had come to reflect the backwardness of Russia and the decline of the working class.

Trotsky's solution to this dilemma was, at first, to persist resolutely along the substitutionalist course.

It is necessary to create amongst us the awareness of the revolutionary historical birthright of the party. The party is obliged to maintain its dictatorship, regardless of temporary wavering in the spontaneous moods of the masses, regardless of the temporary vacillations even in the working class. This awareness is for us the indispensible unifying element.[4]

This attitude led him to argue that the unions ought to be absorbed into the state machine (as later happened under Stalin, in fact though not in form). There was no need or justification for even relative union autonomy; it merely served as a focus for discontent rather than a means of exerting party control.

Lenin's arguments against this position in December 1920 and January 1921 are important for the later development of Trotsky's analysis of the USSR. They were, belatedly, to become its foundation.

Comrade Trotsky speaks of a 'workers' state'. May I say that this is an abstraction. It is natural for us to write about a workers' state in 1917; but it is now a patent error to say 'Since this is a workers' state without any bourgeoisie, against whom then is the working class to be protected

33

and for what purpose?' The whole point is that this is not quite a workers' state. That is where comrade Trotsky makes one of his main mistakes ... [5]

And a month later he wrote:

> What I should have said is: 'A workers' state is an abstraction. What we actually have is a workers' state with this peculiarity, firstly, that it is not the working class but the peasant population that predominates in the country, and, secondly, that it is a workers' state with bureaucratic distortions.'[6]

A bureaucratically distorted workers' state in a predominantly peasant country. In the next stage, the NEP, Trotsky was to adopt this view and to deepen its content. It is not relevant here to describe in detail the fate of the Left Opposition (1923) and the United Opposition (1926-27)[7], in both of which Trotsky played the leading role. Suffice it to present some of their major views.

The left and united oppositions had pressed for the democratisation of the party, the curbing of its apparatus and a planned programme of industrialisation, financed by squeezing the kulak and the Nepman, to combat unemployment, revive the working class economically and politically and so recreate the basis of soviet democracy.

> The material position of the proletariat within the country must be strengthened both absolutely and relatively (growth in the number of employed workers, reduction in the number of unemployed, improvement in the material level of the working class) ...

declared the platform of the Opposition.

> The chronic lagging of industry, and also of transport, electrification and building, behind the demands and needs of the population, of public economy and the social system as a whole, holds as in a vice the entire economic turnover of the country.[8]

34

The inner contradiction of this position was that, on the one hand, to democratise the party would allow both peasant and proletarian discontent to find an organised expression; on the other hand, to increase state pressure on the new rich (especially the richer peasants) would reproduce some of the extreme tensions of war communism that had driven the party, first to suppress all legal extra-party opposition and then to eliminate inner party opposition and establish the dictatorship of the apparatus.

In the event, the matter was not put to the test.

It was not simply the economy that was held 'as in a vice'. The opposition was in like case. Its programme challenged the material interests of all three classes which principally benefitted from the NEP; bureaucrats, Nepmen and kulaks. The opposition could not prevail without that revival of working class activity which was its sole possible basis of support. But that, in turn, was made enormously difficult by the social and economic conditions of the NEP, so long as the revolution remained isolated.

Stalin, chief and spokesman of the conservatised layer of party and state officials who actually ruled the country, vigorously resisted *both* the demand for planned industrialisation and the demand for democratisation (as did his allies on the far right of the party, notably Bukharin and his supporters).

This was the social content of 'Socialism in One Country' advocated by the ruling group from 1925. It was a declaration for the status quo against 'upheavals' of any kind, against revolutionary expectations and an active policy abroad.

As late as April 1924 Stalin himself had summarised what was then still the accepted view:

For the overthrow of the bourgeoisie, the efforts of one country are enough - to this the victory of our own revolution testifies. For the final victory of socialism, for the organisation of socialist production, the efforts of one country, especially a peasant country like ours, are not enough - for this we must have the efforts of the proletarians of several advanced countries.[9]

It was a paraphrase of Lenin and no more than a statement of the social and economic realities. But this orthodox view, once the common property of Russian marxists of all tendencies, had the disadvantage of emphasising the provisional character of the regime and its dependence, for a socialist development, on revolutions in the West. This was now profoundly unacceptable to the ruling layers. 'Socialism in One Country' was their declaration of independence from the workers' movement.

After the final defeat of the Opposition and his exile from Russia Trotsky summed up the experience in an article written in February 1929:

> after the conquest of power, an independent bureaucracy differentiated itself out from the working class milieu and this differentiation... [which] was at first only functional, then later became social. Naturally, the processes within the bureaucracy developed in relation to profound processes under way in the country. On the basis of the New Economic Policy a broad layer of petty bourgeoisie in the towns reappeared or newly came into being. The liberal professions revived. In the countryside, the rich peasant, the kulak, raised his head. Broad sections of officialdom, precisely because they had risen above the masses, drew close to the bourgeois strata and established family ties with them. Increasingly, initiative or criticism on the part of the masses was viewed as interference... The majority of this officialdom which has risen up over the masses is profoundly conservative... This conservative layer, which constitutes Stalin's most powerful support in his struggle against the Opposition, is inclined to go much further to the right, in the direction of the new propertied elements, than Stalin himself or the main nucleus of his faction.[10]

36

The political conclusion drawn from this analysis was the danger of a 'Soviet Thermidor'. On the 9th of Thermidor (27 July 1794) the Jacobin dictatorship was overthrown by the Convention and replaced by a rightist regime (the Directory from 1795) which presided over a political and social reaction in France and paved the way for Bonaparte's dictatorship (from 1799). Thermidor marked the end of the Great French Revolution. A Russian Thermidor now threatened.

> Elements of a Thermidorean process, to be sure one that is completely distinctive, may also be found in the land of the Soviets. They have become strikingly evident in recent years. Those who are in power today either played a secondary role in the decisive events of the first period of the revolution or were outright opponents of the revolution and only joined it after it was victorious. They now serve for the most part as camouflage for those layers and groupings which, while hostile to socialism, are too weak for a counterrevolutionary overturn and therefore seek a peaceful Thermidorean switching back onto the track leading to bourgeois society; they seek to 'roll downhill with the brakes on', as one of their ideologists has put it.[11]

This, however, had not yet happened. Nor was it inevitable. The workers' state was still intact, although eroded. The outcome, Trotsky believed,

> will be decided by the course of the struggle itself as the living forces of society fight it out. There will be ebbs and flows, whose duration will depend to a great extent on the situation in Europe and throughout the world.[12]

To summarise, there were three basic forces at work in the USSR: the forces of the right - the neo-capitalist elements, kulaks, Nepmen, etc., for whom a big section of the apparatus 'in power today' serve 'for the most part as a camouflage'; the working class, represented politically by the now suppressed

37

Opposition; and the 'centrist bureaucracy', Stalin's faction at the top of the machine, which is not itself Thermidorean but which rests on the Thermidoreans and zigzags from left to right in its attempts to hold power.

It had zigged rightwards from 1923 to 1928; then came the left zag. 'The course of 1928-31', Trotsky wrote in the latter year,

> if we again leave aside the inevitable waverings and back-slidings - represents an attempt of the bureaucracy to adapt itself to the proletariat, but without abandoning the principled basis of its policy or, what is most important, its omnipotence. The zigzags of Stalinism show that the bureaucracy is not a class, not an independent historical factor, but an instrument, an executive organ of the classes. The left zigzag is proof that no matter how far the preceding right course has gone, it nevertheless developed on the basis of the dictatorship of the proletariat.[13]

Therefore, the working class still, in some sense, held power - or at least had the possibility of recovering power without a fundamental upheaval.

> The recognition of the present Soviet state as a workers' state not only signifies that the bourgeoisie can conquer power only by means of an armed uprising but also that the proletariat of the USSR has not forfeited the possibility of subordinating the bureaucracy to it, of reviving the party again, and of regenerating the regime of the dictatorship - without a new revolution, with the methods and on the road of *reform*.[14]

By the time this was written it was, factually, without any foundation. The 'three forces' analysis was hopelessly outdated. In the twenties it had been a realistic (if provisional) attempt at a marxist analysis of the course of development in the USSR.

The neo-capitalist classes, and their influence on the right wing of the ruling party, were real enough in 1924-27. The vacillating role of Stalin's ruling faction was, *at that time*, as described. But there had been a *fundamental* change in 1928-29.

By 1928 the NEP was entering its final crisis. Nepmen and kulaks had a vital interest in maintaining it and expanding yet further the concession to petty capitalism, urban and rural. The leading members of the bureaucracy, and their vast clientele in the lower ranks of the bureaucratic hierarchy, had no such vital interest. They had a *vital* interest only in resisting democratisation in party and state. They had allied themselves with the forces of petty capitalism (and the Bukharinist right wing of the party) against the Opposition, against the danger of working class revival.

But when, with the Opposition crushed, the bureaucracy was faced with a kulak offensive, the 'grain strike' of 1927-28, it demonstrated that its essential basis was state property and the state machine, neither of which had any *organic* connection with the NEP. It vigorously defended its interests against its allies of yesterday.

The kulaks controlled practically all the marketable grain, the surplus over and above peasant consumption (the most generally accepted estimate is that one fifth of peasant farmers produced four-fifths of the grain sold on the market). Their attempt to force up prices by withholding their stocks from the market forced the bureaucracy to resort to requisitioning. And once started on this course, which undermined the fundamental basis of the NEP, they were driven to take over the Opposition's industrialisation programme, which they did in a most extravagantly exaggerated form, and to undertake the forced collectivisation of agriculture, the 'liquidation of the kulaks as a class'. The first 'five year plan' was launched.

Trotsky interpreted this as a (temporary) lurch to the left by the Stalinist bureaucracy; as an attempt '*to adapt itself to the proletariat*'. He was profoundly mistaken. These were the very years in which the proletariat in the USSR was atomised and subjected, for the first time, to a truly totalitarian despotism. Real wages fell sharply. Although money wages rose considerably, prices rose much faster. In general, meaningful statistics ceased to be published after 1929 (itself a significant fact) but one calculation, published in the USSR long after the event (1966), showed real wages as 88.6 in 1932 (1928 = 100). 'The correct real wage index, if only we knew it, would ... be well below 88.6', comments Alex Nove, the source of this information.[15]

The five year plan ushered in a period of directing the economy according to an overall plan, of rapid industrial growth, the forcible collectivisation of agriculture, the destruction of the remaining political and trade union rights of the working class, the rapid growth of social inequality, extreme social tension and forced labour on a mass scale. It also heralded Stalin's personal dictatorship and his regime of police terror and, a little later, the murder by shooting or by slow death in the labour camps of the vast majority of the original cadres of the Communist Party and, indeed, of the majority of Stalin's own faction of the twenties, together with an uncertain but *very* large number of other citizens of the USSR and of many foreign communists. In short, it ushered in the high tide of Stalinism.

That Trotsky could initially see all this as a turn to the *left* (although he was not aware of the full facts until some years later) indicates that he had relapsed into substitutionism so far as looking at the USSR was concerned. It was a mistake which he was never able to correct fully. The argument that the bureaucracy was not an independent historical factor but an instrument, an executive organ of other classes, had been decisively refuted when that same bureaucracy simultaneously crushed the kulaks and atomised the workers.

In the early thirties it was still possible to argue about the facts. The newly-born totalitarian regime imposed a blackout of real news and substituted its own monolithic propaganda machine. Trotsky was less deceived by this than almost anyone else. It was his theoretical concept and framework that led him to advocate the prospect of 'reform' in the USSR at this time. A famous, and profoundly misleading, analogy of the USSR with a bureaucratised trade union originated in this period. It was, at least, logically coherent so long as the reform strategy persisted.

The Workers' State, Thermidor and Bonapartism

In October 1933 Trotsky abruptly changed his position, arguing now that the regime could not be reformed. It had to be overthrown. The path of 'reform' was no longer feasible. Only revolution could destroy the bureaucracy:

> After the experiences of the last few years it would be childish to suppose that the Stalinist bureaucracy can be removed by means of a party or soviet congress. In reality, the last congress of the Bolshevik Party took place at the beginning of 1923, the Twelfth Party Congress. All subsequent congresses were bureaucratic parades. Today, even such congresses have been discarded. No normal 'constitutional' ways remain to remove the ruling clique. The bureaucracy can be compelled to yield power into the hands of the proletarian vanguard only by force.[16]

The 'bureaucratised trade union' had to be *smashed*, not reformed. It is true that this article contains the statement: 'Today the rupture of the bureaucratic equilibrium in the USSR would almost surely serve in favour of the counter-revolutionary forces', but this equivocal position soon gave way to a revolutionary one.

With characteristic honesty, Trotsky went on to criticise and revise his own earlier 'reformist' perspective, writing in 1935 that:

> The question of 'Thermidor' is closely bound up with the history of the Left Opposition in the USSR . . . In any case

the positions on this issue in 1926 were approximately as follows: the group of 'Democratic Centralism' (V.M. Smirnov, Sapronov and others who were hounded to death in exile by Stalin) declared 'Thermidor is an accomplished fact.' The adherents of the platform of the Left Opposition ... categorically denied this assertion ... Who has proved to be correct? ...

The late V.M. Smirnov - one of the finest representatives of the Old Bolshevik school - held that the lag in industrialisation, the growth of the kulak and of the Nepman (the new bourgeois), the liaison between the bureaucracy and the latter and, finally, the degeneration of the party, had progressed so far as to render impossible a return to the socialist road without a new revolution. The proletariat had already lost power ... The fundamental conquests of the October revolution had been liquidated.[17]

Trotsky's conclusion was:

The Thermidor of the Great Russian Revolution is not before us but already far behind. The Thermidoreans can celebrate, approximately, the tenth anniversary of their victory. [That is, it had occurred around 1925.][18]

So had the democratic centralists been right in 1926? Yes and no, Trotsky now said. Right about the Thermidor, wrong about its significance. 'The present political regime in the USSR is a regime of "Soviet" (or anti-Soviet) Bonapartism, closer in type to the empire rather than the Consulate.' *But*, he continued, 'In its social foundations and economic tendencies the USSR remains a workers' state.'[18]

In terms of formal analogies all this was plausible enough. As Trotsky pointed out, both the Thermidoreans and Bonaparte represented a *reaction* on the basis of the bourgeois revolution, not a return to the *ancien regime*. The fact remains that Trotsky, no less than Smirnov, had previously considered the 'Soviet Thermidor' in a fundamentally different light. 'The proletariat had already lost power' was the essence of Smirnov's thesis, and that Trotsky strongly denied at the time. For him, the party, however bureaucratised, still represented the working class. The working class, unlike the bourgeoisie, could only hold power through its organisations.

'Comrades', he had declared in 1924,

> none of us wishes to be or can be right against the party. In the last instance the party is always right, because it is the only historic instrument which the working class possesses for the solution of its fundamental tasks... One can be right only with the party and through the party because history has not created any other way for the realisation of one's rightness... The English have the saying 'My country right or wrong'. With much greater justification we can say: My party, right or wrong - wrong on certain specific issues or at certain moments.[19]

But the party - the Russian party - had become the instrument first of Thermidor and now Bonapartism; that was Trotsky's position at the end of 1933. Since the party had ceased to be an instrument of the working class - its regime had to be overthrown 'by force' - and since, admittedly, the Russian workers had no other instrument (were in fact atomised and terrorised) what could be left of the workers' state?

Nothing. That was the only possible conclusion if the terms were to retain the meaning everyone had taken for granted till then. A new revolution, 'a victorious revolutionary uprising', was necessary for the working class to regain power in the USSR. The working class had lost power and there was no peaceful, constitutional way for it to capture power again. Therefore the workers' state no longer existed. A counter-revolution had taken place.

Trotsky firmly rejected these conclusions. He was therefore forced to make a fundamental shift in his definition of a workers' state.

The *social* domination of a class (its dictatorship) may find extremely diverse *political* forms. This is attested by the entire history of the bourgeoisie from the Middle Ages to the present day. The experience of the Soviet Union is already adequate for the extension of this sociological law - *with all the necessary changes* - to the dictatorship of the proletariat as well ... Thus the present day domination of Stalin in no way resembles the Soviet rule during the initial years of the revolution ... But this usurpation was made possible only because *the social content of the dictatorship of the bureaucracy is determined by those productive relations that were created by the proletarian revolution.* In this sense we may say with complete justification that the dictatorship of the proletariat found its distorted but indubitable expression in the dictatorship of the bureaucracy.[20]

Trotsky held this position in essence, for the last half decade of his life. His book *The Revolution Betrayed* (1937) elaborates it with a wealth of detail and vivid illustration.

The *fundamental* nature of the break with his own earlier views can hardly be overstated. It was one thing to argue (as Lenin had done) that a workers' state could be bureaucratically distorted, deformed, degenerated or whatever. Now what was being asserted was that the dictatorship of the proletariat had no *necessary* connection with any actual workers' power at all. The dictatorship of the proletariat now came to mean, first and foremost, state ownership of industry and economic planning (although planning hardly existed under the NEP); it could remain extant even if the working class was atomised and subjected to a totalitarian despotism.

It must be said in Trotsky's favour that he was dealing with an entirely new phenomenon. He, like all the oppositionists in the twenties, had seen the danger of a collapse of the regime due to pressure from the growing forces of petty capitalism. That was what Thermidor had meant to all of them. The actual outcome was quite unexpected. State property not only survived but expanded rapidly. The bureaucracy did *in fact* play an independent role, a fact Trotsky would never fully admit. The resulting regime was, at that time, unique.

No restoration of the bourgeoisie had taken place. Moreover, at a time of profound industrial depression in the West, rapid economic growth occurred in the USSR, a point Trotsky repeatedly emphasised in support of his contention that the regime was not capitalist.

Prognosis

In his 1938 *Transitional Programme* Trotsky wrote:

The Soviet Union emerged from the October revolution as a workers' state. State ownership of the means of production, a necessary prerequisite to socialist development, opened up the possibility of rapid growth of the productive forces. But the apparatus of the workers' state underwent a complete degeneration at the same time: it was transformed from a weapon of the working class into a weapon of bureaucratic violence against the working class, and more and more a weapon for the sabotage of the country's economy. The bureaucratisation of a backward and isolated workers' state and the transformation of the bureaucracy into an all-powerful privileged caste constitute the most convincing refutation - not only theoretically but this time practically - of the theory of socialism in one country.

The USSR thus embodied terrific contradictions. But it still remained a *degenerated workers' state*. Such is the social diagnosis. The political prognosis has an alternative character: either the bureaucracy, becoming ever more the organ of the world bourgeoisie within the workers' state, will overthrow the new forms of property and plunge the country back to capitalism; or the working class will crush the bureaucracy and open the way to socialism.[21]

Why should this be so? Trotsky was convinced that the bureaucracy was highly unstable and politically heterogeneous. All sorts of tendencies 'from genuine Bolshevism to complete fascism' existed within it, he claimed in 1938. These tendencies were related to social forces, including

> conscious capitalist tendencies . . . mainly the prosperous part of the collective farms . . . [which] provides itself with a wide base for petty bourgeois tendencies of accumulating personal wealth at the expense of general poverty, and are consciously encouraged by the bureaucracy.[22]

Within the bureaucracy,

> fascist, counterrevolutionary elements, growing uninterruptedly, express with ever greater consistency, the interests of world imperialism. These candidates for the role of compradores consider, not without reason, that the new ruling layer can ensure their positions of privilege only through rejection of nationalisation, collectivisation and monopoly of foreign trade in the name of the assimilation of 'Western civilisation, i.e., capitalism . . . Atop this system of mounting antagonism, trespassing ever more on the social equilibrium, the Thermidorean oligarchy, today reduced mainly to Stalin's Bonapartist clique, hangs on by terroristic methods . . . The extermination of the generation of Old Bolsheviks and of the revolutionary representatives of the middle and young generations has acted to disrupt the political equilibrium still more in favour of the right, bourgeois, wing of the bureaucracy, and of its allies throughout the land. From them, i.e., from the right, we can expect ever more determined attempts in the next period to revise the socialist character of the USSR and bring it closer to the pattern of 'Western civilisation' in its fascist form.[23]

It is interesting that Trotsky at this time should draw attention to the similarities between fascism and Stalinism, when the Popular Front was still at its height. 'Stalinism and fascism, in spite of a deep difference in social foundation, are symmetrical phenomena. In many of their features they show a deadly similarity,' he wrote in *The Revolution Betrayed*.[24] And again 'As in the fascist countries, from which Stalin's *political* apparatus does not differ save in more unbridled savagery . . . ' [25] What they have in common - the destruction of each and every independent workers' organisation and the atomisation of the working class - is very striking. But, on the assumption that there was a 'deep difference in social foundations', had a *fascist* workers' state come into being?

Most important, however, is the question of the 'restorationist' tendencies of the bureaucracy. There is no substantial argument in Trotsky's writings at this period, other than that on the right of inheritance:

> Privileges are only half their worth if they cannot be transmitted to one's children. But the right of testament is inseparable from the right of property. It is not enough to be the director of a trust; it is necessary to be a stockholder.[26]

thus demonstrating the pressure on the bureaucracy to abandon its own control of the USSR in favour of becoming junior partners (compradores) of the various imperialist powers.

In Trotsky's view, the Soviet Union, was still 'a contradictory society halfway between capitalism and socialism . . . In the last analysis, the question [forward to socialism or back to capitalism] will be decided by a struggle of living social forces, both in the national and the world arena.'

That struggle had already developed in such a way as to strain Trotsky's analysis to the very limits in the last years before his death.

3. Strategy and Tactics

The ideal of an international workers' movement is as old as, if not indeed older than, the Communist Manifesto itself, with its call, 'Workers of the world unite'. In 1864 (the First International) and again in 1889 (the Second International) attempts had been made to give it an organisational expression. The Second International had collapsed in 1914 when its big parties in the warring states broke with internationalism and supported the governments of the German and Austrian Kaisers, the English king and the French bourgeois Third Republic.

It was not that they had been taken by surprise. Pre-war congresses had repeatedly drawn attention to the menace of imperialism and militarism, the growing threat of war and the need for the workers' parties to stand firm against their own governments, indeed to 'utilise the crisis engendered by war to hasten the downfall of capitalist class rule', as the Stuttgart Congress of the International had put it in 1907.

The subsequent capitulations of 1914, a stunning defeat for the socialist movement, led Lenin to declare: 'The Second International is dead . . . Long live the Third International'. Five years later, in 1919, the Third International was actually founded. Trotsky played a major role in it in the early years.

Later, with the rise of Stalinism in the USSR, the International was prostituted in the service of the Stalinist state in Russia. Trotsky more than anyone else fought against this degeneration. Many of his most valuable writings on the strategy and tactics of revolutionary workers' parties relate to the Third International, the Comintern, both in the period of its rise and in the period of its subsequent decline.

> Sweeping aside the half-heartedness, lies and corruption of the outlived official Socialist parties, we Communists, united in the Third International, consider ourselves the direct continuators of the heroic endeavours and martyrdom of a long line of revolutionary generations from Babeuf to Karl Liebknecht and Rosa Luxemburg.
>
> If the First International presaged the future course of development and indicated its paths; if the Second International gathered and organised millions of workers; then the Third International is the International of open mass action, the International of revolutionary realisation, the International of the deed.[1]

Trotsky was forty and at the height of his power when he wrote the *Manifesto of the Communist International* from which the above lines are taken. As the People's Commissar for War of the embattled Soviet Republic, he was second only to Lenin as the recognised spokesman of world communism.

His outlook at this time was not, of course, especially distinctive. It was the common outlook of the whole Bolshevik leadership, an outlook which did not exclude sharp differences of opinion on this or that issue but which was essentially homogeneous. However, Trotsky was to become in time the outstanding advocate of the ideas of the Communist International in its heroic period. Events, unforeseen by any of the revolutionary leaders of 1919 - or by their opponents - later reduced to a handful the bearers of this authentic communist tradition; Trotsky came to tower over them as a giant among Lilliputians.

Time and again, in his writings in the late twenties and the thirties, Trotsky was to refer to the decisions of the first four congresses of the Comintern as the model of revolutionary policy. What were these decisions and in what circumstances were they adopted?

It was 4 March 1919. Thirty-five delegates meeting in the Kremlin voted, with one abstention, to constitute the Third or

Communist International. It was not a very weighty or representative gathering. Only the five delegates from the Russian Communist Party (Bukharin, Chicherin, Lenin, Trotsky and Zinoviev) represented a party which was both a mass organisation and a genuinely revolutionary one. Stange of the Norwegian Labour Party (NAP) came from a mass party but, as events were to prove, the NAP was far from revolutionary in practice. Eberlein of the newly-formed Communist Party of Germany (KPD) represented a real revolutionary organisation but one that was still only a few thousand strong. Most of the other delegates represented very little.

The majority took it for granted that an 'International' without some real mass support in a number of countries was nonsense. Zinoviev, for the Russians, argued that mass support existed in fact. The weakness of many of the delegations was accidental. 'We have a victorious proletarian revolution in a great country... You have in Germany a party marching to power which in a few months will establish a proletarian government. And are we still to delay? No one will understand it.'[2]

That the socialist revolution was an immediate prospect in central Europe, above all in Germany, was not doubted by any of the delegates. In Eberlein's words: 'Unless all the signs are deceptive, the German proletariat is facing the last decisive struggle. However difficult it may be, the prospects for communism are favourable.[3]

Lenin, the most sober and calculating of revolutionaries, had said in his opening speech that 'not only in Russia, but in the most developed capitalist countries of Europe, Germany for example, civil war is a fact... the world revolution is beginning and growing in intensity everywhere.'[4]

This was not fantasy. In November 1918 the German Empire, till then the most powerful state in Europe, had collapsed. Six people's commissars - three social democrats and three independent social democrats - replaced the Kaiser's government. Workers' and soldiers' councils had covered the country and wielded effective power. True, the social-democratic leaders, who dominated them, bent all their efforts towards reconstituting the old capitalist state power under a new 'republican' guise. That was all the more reason for creating a revolutionary International with a strong centralised leadership to guide and support the struggle for a Soviet Germany. And that struggle, in spite of the bloody suppression of the Spartakus rising in January 1919, appeared to be developing. 'From January to May 1919, with offshoots reaching into the height of the summer, a bloody civil war was waged in Germany . . . '[5] A month after the Moscow meeting the Bavarian Soviet Republic was proclaimed.

The other great central European power, the Austro-Hungarian Empire, had ceased to exist. The successor states were in varying degrees of revolutionary ferment. In German-speaking Austria the only effective armed force was the social-democratic controlled Volkswehr (People's Army). In Hungary, the Soviet Republic was proclaimed on 21 March 1919. All the new or reconstituted states - Czechoslovakia, Yugoslavia, even Poland - were highly unstable.

The role of the socialist leaderships was crucial. The majority now supported counter-revolution in the name of 'democracy'. Most of them claimed to be, indeed once had been, marxists and internationalists. In 1914 they had capitulated to 'their own' ruling classes. They were now, in this critical time, *the* major prop of capitalism, using socialist phrases and the credit established by their years of opposition to the old regimes before 1914 to prevent the establishment of workers' power. Their attempt to reconstitute the Second International at a meeting in Berne was advanced as a further, urgent reason for proclaiming the Third. As early as 1914 Lenin had written: 'The Second International is dead, overcome by opportunism . . . long live the Third International.'[6] Now, eighteen months after the October revolution, the slogan was to be turned into reality.

What was its essential political basis? It rested on two

fundamental planks; revolutionary internationalism and the soviet system as the means whereby the workers would rule society.

The main resolution of the 1919 Congress declared:

> Democracy assumed different forms and was applied in different degrees in the ancient republics of Greece, the medieval cities and the advanced capitalist countries. It would be sheer nonsense to think that the most profound revolution in history, the first case in the world of power being transferred from the exploiting minority to the exploited majority, could take place within the time worn framework of the old, bourgeois parliamentary democracy, without drastic changes, without the creation of new forms of democracy, new institutions that embody the new conditions for applying democracy.[7]

Soviets or parliament? After the October revolution the Russian Communist Party had dispersed the newly elected Constituent Assembly, in which the Social-Revolutionary peasant party had a majority, in favour of soviet power. After the November revolution the German Social-Democratic Party had dissolved the workers' and soldiers' councils, in which it had a majority, in favour of the National Assembly in which it did not.

In both cases the question of constitutional forms was really a question of class power. The effect of the RCP's action was to create a workers' state. The effect of the SPD's action was to create a bourgeois state, the Weimar Republic.

Marx had written, after the Paris Commune, that in the transition from capitalism to socialism, the form of the state 'can only be the revolutionary dictatorship of the proletariat'.

The social-democrats had come, in practice, to reject the essence of the marxist theory of the state, that *all* states are class states, that there is no 'neutral' state. They had come to reject their own previous position on the inevitability of revolution in favour of 'peaceful' parliamentary roads to socialism.

52

Yet the Weimar Republic was every bit as much a product of the violent overthrow of the previous state as the Russian Soviet Republic had been. Mutinous soldiers and armed workers, not voters, overthrew the German Empire. The same was true of the successor states of Austria-Hungary. But the greater transformation, the destruction of capitalism, was to be achieved by the ordinary mechanisms of bourgeois democracy!

In reality, this meant the abandonment of socialism as the aim.

The Third International, in its 1919 'platform', sharply restated the marxist position. 'The victory of the working class lies in shattering the organisation of the enemy power and organising workers' power; it consists in the destruction of the bourgeois state machine and the construction of the workers' state machine.'[8] There could be no question of socialism through parliament. Lenin, in 1917, had quoted with approval Engels's statement that universal suffrage is 'an index of the maturity of the working class. It cannot and never will be anything more in a modern state'.[9] 'No bourgeois republic, however democratic,' he wrote just after the Moscow conference, 'ever was or could have been anything but a machine for the repression of the working people by capital, an instrument of the dictatorship of the bourgeoisie, the political rule of capital.'[10]

The workers' republic, based on workers' councils, was truly democratic.

> The essence of soviet power lies in this, that the permanent and sole foundation of the entire state power, of the entire state apparatus, is the mass organisation of those very classes which were oppressed by the capitalists, that is the workers and semi-workers (peasants who do not exploit labour).[11]

This was something of an idealisation of Russia, even in 1919, but the 'deviations' were accounted for by the backwardness of the country, the still raging civil war and foreign intervention.

Trotsky then, and until his dying day, supported all these ideas without the slightest reservation. He was at one with Lenin on the questions of bourgeois democracy and reformism in 1919, and he never changed his mind.

The delegates' meeting in Moscow had constituted the new International on the basis of uncompromising internationalism, a decisive and final split with the traitors of 1914, workers' power, workers' councils, the defence of the Soviet Republic and the perspective of revolution in the near future in Central and Western Europe. The problem now was to create the mass parties that could make all this a reality.

Centrism and Ultra-Leftism

Parties and groups only recently affiliated to the Second International are more and more frequently applying for membership in the Third International, though they have not become really communist...The Communist International is, to a certain extent, becoming fashionable... In certain circumstances, the Communist International may be faced with the danger of dilution by the influx of wavering and irresolute groups that have not yet broken with their Second International ideology.[12]

So wrote Lenin in July 1920. The assumption of the 1919 Congress of the Comintern, that a truly *mass* revolutionary movement existed in Europe, was shown to be correct in the coming year.

In September 1919 the Bologna congress of the Italian Socialist Party voted by a large majority and on the recommendation of its executive to affiliate to the Communist International. The Norwegian Labour Party, the NAP, confirmed its affiliation and the Bulgarian, Yugoslav (ex-Serbian) and Rumanian parties joined as well. The first three of these were important organisations. The NAP which, like its British counterpart, was based on trade union affiliation, completely

54

dominated the Norwegian left, and the Bulgarian CP had the support from the beginning of virtually the whole Bulgarian working class. The Yugoslavian CP returned 54 deputies in the first (and only) free elections held in the new state.

In France, the Socialist Party, SFIO, which had more than doubled its membership - from 90,000 to 200,000 between 1918 and 1920 - had swung far to the left, and was flirting with Moscow. So were the leaders of the German Independent Social Democrats, the USPD, an organisation which was rapidly gaining ground at the expense of the Social Democratic Party, the SPD. The Swedish left Social-Democrats, the Czechoslovak left wing and smaller parties in other countries (including the British ILP) had essentially the same line. Pressure from their ranks was forcing them to pay lip service to the October revolution and to negotiate for admission to the Communist International.

'The desire of certain leading "centre" groups to join the Third International', wrote Lenin, 'provides indirect confirmation that it has won the sympathy of the vast majority of class conscious workers throughout the world, and is becoming a more powerful force with each day.'[13]

But these parties were not revolutionary communist organisations. Their traditions were those of pre-war social-democracy - revolutionary in words, passive in practice. And they were led by men who would try any twist or turn in order to keep control and prevent the adoption of genuine revolutionary strategy and tactics.

Without the bulk of the members of these parties the new International could not hope to exert a decisive influence in Europe in the short term. Without a break with the centrist leaders it could not hope to exert a *revolutionary* influence. Nor was the situation much different with the mass parties already inside the International. The Italian Socialist Party, for example, had centrists and even some thorough-going reformists in its leadership.

The struggle against centrism was complicated by another

factor. Strong ultra-leftist currents existed inside many of the communist organisations. And outside them were some important syndicalist trade union organisations which had moved close to the Third International but which still rejected the need for a communist party. To gain and integrate these big forces was a difficult and complex operation. It required a struggle on several different fronts.

The decisions of the Second Congress were of fundamental importance. In a sense this was the real founding congress. It took place during the height of the war with Poland, when the Red Army was nearing Warsaw. In Germany an attempt to establish a military dictatorship, the Kapp putsch, had just been defeated by mass working class action. In Italy the factory occupations were about to begin. The mood of revolutionary optimism was stronger than ever. Zinoviev, President of the International, declared: 'I am deeply convinced that the Second World Congress of the CI is the precursor of another world congress, the world congress of Soviet Republics.'[14] All that was needed were real mass communist parties to lead the movement to victory. One of Trotsky's major interventions in the congress was concerned with the *nature* of such parties.

Comrades, it may seem fairly strange that three-quarters of a century after the appearance of the *Communist Manifesto*, discussion should arise at an International Communist Congress over whether a party is necessary or not . . . It is self-evident that if we were dealing here with Messrs. Scheidemann, Kautsky or their English co-thinkers, it would not, of course, be necessary to convince these gentlemen that a party is indispensable for the working class. They have created a party for the working class and handed it over into the service of bourgeois and capitalist society . . . Just because I know that the party is indispensable, and am well aware of the value of the party, and just because I see Scheidemann on the one side and, on the other, American or Spanish or French syndicalists who not only wish to fight against the bourgeoisie but who, unlike Scheidemann, really want to tear its head off - for this reason I say that I prefer to discuss with these Spanish, American and French comrades in order to prove to them that the party is indispensible for the fulfilment of the mission which is placed upon them - the destruction of the bourgeoisie...Comrades, the French syndicalists are conducting revolutionary work within the unions. When I discuss today, for example, with Comrade Rosmer, we have a common ground. The French syndicalists, in defiance of the traditions of democracy and its deceptions, have said: 'We do not want any parties, we stand for proletarian unions and for the revolutionary minority within them which applies direct action...' What does this minority mean to our friends? It is the chosen section of the French working class, a section with a clear programme and organisation of its own, an organisation where they discuss all questions, and not alone discuss but also decide, and where they are bound by a certain discipline.[15]

This, Trotsky argued, was the root of the matter. The revolutionary syndicalists were much closer to constituting a *communist* party than the centrists who took the idea of a party for granted. The syndicalist position was not entirely adequate - something had to be added: 'an inventory...which concentrates the entire experience accumulated by the working class. That is how we conceive our party. That is how we conceive our International.'[16]

It could not be primarily a propaganda organisation. Speaking at the Comintern Executive (ECCI) against the Dutch ultra-left Gorter who had accused the Comintern of 'chasing after the masses', Trotsky declared:

What does Comrade Gorter propose? What does he want? Propaganda! This is the gist of his entire method.

Revolution, says Comrade Gorter, is contingent neither upon privations nor economic conditions but on mass consciousness; while mass consciousness is, in turn, shaped by propaganda. Propaganda is here taken in a purely idealistic manner, very much akin to the concept of the eighteenth century school of enlightenment and rationalism ... What you now want to do amounts essentially to replacing the dynamic development of the International by methods of individual recruitment of workers through propaganda. You want some sort of simon-pure International of the elect and select ... [17]

The passive, propagandist type of ultra-leftism was not the only variety represented in the early Comintern. In 1921, a putschist tendency developed in the leadership of the German party. In March of that year, in the absence of a revolutionary situation nationally (locally, in parts of central Germany, something like a revolutionary situation existed), the party leadership tried to force the pace, to *substitute* the party militants for a true mass movement. The result of this 'March Action' was a serious defeat - party membership dropped from about 350,000 to around 150,000. A 'theory of the offensive' was used to justify the KPD tactics.

There was advanced the so-called theory of the offensive. What is the gist of this theory? Its gist is that we have entered the epoch of the decomposition of capitalist society, in other words, the epoch when the bourgeoisie must be overthrown. How? By the offensive of the working class. In this purely abstract form it is unquestionably correct. But certain individuals have sought to convert this theoretical capital into corresponding currency of smaller denominations and they have declared that this offensive consists of a successive number of smaller offensives ...

noted Trotsky in a speech in the summer of 1921. He went on:

Comrades, the analogy between the political struggle of the working class and military operations has been much abused. But up to a certain point one can speak here of similarities . . . In military respects we, too, had our March days, speaking in German and our September days, speaking in Italian [the reference is to the failure of the Italian Socialist Party to exploit the revolutionary crisis of September 1920]. What happens after a partial defeat? There sets in a certain dislocation of the military apparatus, there arises a certain need for a breathing spell, a need for reorientation and a more precise estimation of the reciprocal forces . . . Sometimes all this becomes possible only under the conditions of strategic retreat . . .

But to understand this properly, to discern in a move backwards, in a retreat, a component part of a unified strategic plan - for that a certain experience is necessary. But if one reasons purely abstractly and insists on always moving forward . . . on the assumption that everything can be superseded by an added extension of revolutionary will, what results does one then get? Let us take for example the September events in Italy or the March events in Germany. We are told that the situation in these countries can be remedied only by a new offensive . . . Under these conditions we would suffer an even greater and much more dangerous defeat. No comrades, after such a defeat we must retreat.[18]

The United Front
In fact, by the summer of 1921, the Comintern leadership had decided that a strategic retreat in a more general sense was necessary. Trotsky wrote in *Pravda* in June:

In the most critical year for the bourgeoisie, the year 1919, the proletariat of Europe could undoubtedly have conquered state power with minimum sacrifices, had there been at its head a genuine revolutionary organisation, setting forth clear aims and capably pursuing them, i.e., a strong Communist Party. But there was none... During the last three years the workers have fought a great deal and suffered many sacrifices. But they have not won power. As a result the working masses have become more cautious than they were in 1919-20.[19]

The same thought was expressed in the *Theses on the World Situation*, of which Trotsky was the author, adopted at the Third Comintern Congress in July 1921:

During the year that has passed between the second and third congresses of the Communist International, a series of working-class risings and struggles have ended in partial defeat (the advance of the Red Army on Warsaw in August 1920, the movement of the Italian proletariat in September 1920, the rising of the German workers in March 1921.) The first period of the post-war revolutionary movement, distinguished by the spontaneous character of its assaults, by the marked imprecision of its aims and methods, and by the extreme panic which it aroused amongst the ruling classes, seems in essentials to be over. The self-confidence of the bourgeoisie as a class, and the outward stability of their state organs, have undeniably been strengthened... The leaders of the bourgeoisie are even boasting of the power of their state machines and have gone over to an offensive against the workers in all countries both on the economic and on the political front.[20]

Soon after the congress, the ECCI began to press the parties to shift the emphasis of their work towards the united front. The essence of this approach was very clearly summarised by Trotsky early in 1922.

The task of the Communist Party is to lead the proletarian revolution... to achieve it the Communist Party must base itself on the overwhelming majority of the working class... The party can achieve this only by remaining an absolutely independent organisation with a clear programme and strict internal discipline. That is why the party was bound to break ideologically with the reformists and centrists... After assuring itself of the complete independence and ideological homogeneity of its ranks, the Communist Party fights for influence over the majority of the working class... But it is perfectly self-evident that the class life of the proletariat is not suspended during this period preparatory to the revolution. Clashes with industrialists, with the bourgeoisie, with the state power, on the initiative of one side or the other, run their due course.

In these clashes - insofar as they involve the vital interests of the entire working class, or its majority, or this or that section - the working masses sense the need of unity in action, of unity in resisting the onslaught of capitalism or unity in taking the offensive against it. Any party which mechanically counterposes itself to this need of the working class for unity in action will unfailingly be condemned in the minds of the workers.

Consequently the question of the united front is not at all, either in point of origin or substance, a question of the reciprocal relations between the Communist parliamentary fraction and that of the Socialists, or between the Central Committees of the two parties... The problem of the united front - *despite the fact that a split is inevitable in this epoch between the various political organisations basing themselves on the working class* - grows out of the urgent need to secure for the working class the possibility of a united front in the struggle against capitalism.

For those who do not understand this task, the party is only a propaganda society and not an organisation for mass action...

Unity of front consequently presupposes our readiness, within certain limits and on specific issues, to correlate in practice our actions with those of reformist organisations, to the extent to which the latter still express today the will of important sections of the embattled proletariat.

But, after all, didn't we split with them? Yes, because we disagree with them on fundamental questions of the working class movement.

And yet we seek agreement with them? Yes, in all those cases where the masses that follow them are ready to engage in joint struggle together with the masses that follow us and when they, the reformists, are to a lesser or greater degree compelled to become an instrument of this struggle . . .

A policy aimed to secure the united front does not of course contain automatic guarantees that unity in action will actually be attained in all instances. On the contrary, in many cases and perhaps even the majority of cases, organisational agreements will be only half-attained or perhaps not at all. But it is necessary that the struggling masses should always be given the opportunity of convincing themselves that the non-achievement of unity in action was not due to our formalistic irreconcilability but to the lack of real will to struggle on the part of the reformists.[21]

The Fourth Comintern Congress (1922), which was largely concerned with the united front, was the last Lenin attended and the last which Trotsky regarded as essentially correct in its decisions. A decade later, in a statement of fundamental principles he summarised his attitude to the experience of the early Comintern:

The International Left Opposition stands on the ground of the first four congresses of the Comintern. This does not mean that it bows before every letter of its decisions, many of which had a purely conjunctural character and have been contradicted by subsequent events. But all the essential principles (in relation to imperialism and the bourgeois state, to democracy and reformism; problems of insurrection; the dictatorship of the proletariat; on relations with the peasantry and the oppressed nations; work in the trade unions; parliamentarianism; the policy of the united front) remain, even today, the highest expression of proletarian strategy in the epoch of the general crisis of capitalism. The Left Opposition rejects the revisionist decisions of the Fifth and Sixth World Congresses... [1924 and 1928][22]

1923 saw the emergence of the triumvirate of Stalin, Zinoviev and Kamenev on the one hand and of the Left Opposition on the other. In Europe it saw two crippling defeats for the Comintern. In June, the Bulgarian Communist Party, a mass party enjoying the support of virtually the entire working class, adopted a position of 'neutrality', or rather complete passivity, in the face of the right wing coup against the Peasant Party government. Then, after the bourgeois democratic regime had been destroyed, a military dictatorship established and the mass of the population cowed, it launched (on 22 September) a sudden insurrection, without any serious political preparation. It was smashed and a ferocious White Terror ensued. In Germany, a profound economic, social and political crisis occurred, precipitated by the French occupation of the Ruhr and the astronomic inflation which, literally, made money worthless. 'In the autumn of 1923 the German situation was more desperate than at any time since 1919, the misery greater, the prospect apparently more hopeless.'[23] A rising was planned for October, after the Communist Party had formed a coalition government with Social Democrats in Saxony, but cancelled at the last minute. (In Hamburg the cancellation was not received in time; an isolated insurrection occurred and was crushed after two days.)

Trotsky believed that a historic opportunity had been missed. From this time on the policy of the Comintern became increasingly determined, first by the requirements of Stalin's faction in the inner party struggle in the USSR and later by the foreign policy requirements of Stalin's government. After a brief 'left' oscillation in 1924, the Comintern was pushed in a rightist direction until 1928, then into ultra-leftism (1928-34) and finally far to the right in the Popular Front period (1935-39). Each of these phases was analysed and criticised by Trotsky. It is convenient to present his critique using three examples.

The Anglo-Soviet Trade Union Committee

Aside from the Chinese Revolution of 1925-27, which has already been discussed, the policy (under Comintern direction) of the Communist Party of Great Britain (CPGB) up to and during the general strike of 1926 was the most important indictment Trotsky made of the Comintern in its first rightist phase.

The general strike of May 1926 was a decisive turning point in British history - and it was an unmitigated defeat for the working class. It brought to an end a long, though not uninterrupted, period of working class militancy, it led to the prolonged dominance of the unions by their openly class-collaborationist right wing and it led to the massive reinforcement of Labour Party reformism at the expense of the Communist Party.

In 1924-25 the tide in the trade union movement was flowing leftwards. The CP-inspired Minority Movement, founded in 1924 around the slogans 'Stop the Retreat' and 'Back to the Unions', was gaining considerable influence. At the same time the official movement was coming under the influence of a group of leftish officials. And, from the spring of 1925, the Trades Union Congress (TUC) collaborated with the Soviet Trade Union Federation through the 'Anglo-Soviet Joint Trade Union Advisory Committee', a fact that gave the

General Councillors a certain 'revolutionary' aura and a cover against critics on the left.

The essence of Trotsky's criticism was that the CPGB, on Moscow's urging, was building up trust in these left bureaucrats (the central CP slogan was 'All Power to the General Council'!) who were certain to betray the movement at a critical stage (as they did, of course), rather than struggle to build independently amongst the rank and file, using whatever cover the 'lefts' afforded but in no way relying on them or encouraging militants to rely on them; on the contrary, counting on their treachery, warning against it and preparing for it. Trotsky wrote later:

> Zinoviev gave us to understand that he counted upon the revolution finding an entrance, not through the narrow gateway of the British Communist Party, but through the broad portals of the trade unions. The struggle to win the masses organised in the trade unions through the communist party was replaced by the hope for the swiftest possible utilisation of the ready-made apparatus of the trade unions for the purposes of the revolution. Out of this false position sprang the later policy of the Anglo-Russian Committee which dealt a blow to the Soviet Union, as well as to the British working class; a blow surpassed only by the defeat in China ... As the upshot of the greatest revolutionary movement in Britain since the days of Chartism, the British Communist Party has hardly grown while the General Council sits in the saddle even more firmly than before the general strike. Such are the results of this unique 'strategical manoeuvre'.[24]

He did not argue that the policy of independent communist work would necessarily have won the strike.

> No revolutionist who weighs his words would contend that a victory *would have been guaranteed* by proceeding along this line. But a victory was *possible* only along this road.

A defeat on this road was a defeat on a road that could lead *later* to victory.[25]

However, this road

appeared too long and uncertain to the bureaucrats of the Communist International. They considered that by means of personal influence on Purcell, Hicks, Cook and the others ... they would gradually and imperceptibly draw ... [them] into the Communist International. To guarantee such a success ... the dear friends (Purcell, Hicks and Cook) were not to be vexed or exasperated ... a radical measure had to be resorted to ... actually subordinating the Communist Party to the Minority Movement ... The masses knew as the leaders of this movement only Purcell, Hicks and Cook, whom, moreover, Moscow vouched for. These 'left' friends, in a serious test, shamefully betrayed the proletariat. The revolutionary workers were thrown into confusion, sank into apathy and naturally extended their disappointment to the Communist Party itself which had only been the passive part of this whole mechanism of betrayal and perfidy. The Minority Movement was reduced to zero; the Communist Party returned to the existence of a negligible sect.[26]

Reliance on 'left' officials is still one of the features distinguishing left reformists from revolutionaries. Trotsky's critique is highly relevant today; not least in Britain.

Germany in the Third Period

The Sixth World Congress of the Comintern (summer 1928) began a process of violent reaction against the rightist line of 1924-28. An ultra-leftist line of a peculiarly bureaucratic character was imposed on Communist parties everywhere, regardless of local circumstances. A reflection of the launching of the first five year plan and the forced collectivisation in the USSR, this new line proclaimed a 'Third Period', a period of 'ascending revolutionary struggles.' In practice this meant that at a time when fascism was a real and growing danger, especially in Germany, the social democrats were regarded as the main enemy.

In this situation of growing imperialist contradictions and sharpening of the class struggle,

declared the Tenth Plenum of the ECCI in 1929,

fascism becomes more and more the dominant method of bourgeois rule. In countries where there are strong social-democratic parties, fascism assumes the particular form of social fascism, which to an ever increasing extent serves the bourgeoisie as an instrument for paralysing the activity of the masses in the struggle against the regime of fascist dictatorship.[27]

It followed that the united front policy, as understood until then, had to be jettisoned. There could be no question of trying to force the mass social-democratic parties and the unions they controlled into a united front against the fascists. They were themselves social-fascists. Indeed, added the Eleventh Plenum of the ECCI (1931), social democracy 'is the most active factor and pacemaker in the development of the capitalist state towards fascism'.[28]

This grotesquely false estimate of the nature of both fascism and social democracy led to the assumption that 'strong social-democratic parties' and 'a regime of fascist dictatorship' could co-exist and indeed *did* coexist in Germany well before Hitler came to power. 'In Germany the Von Papen-Schleicher government, with the help of the Reichswehr, the Stahlhelm and the Nazis has established a form of fascist dictatorship ... ',[29] proclaimed the Twelfth Plenum of the ECCI in 1932.

Trotsky wrote and argued against this criminal stupidity with increasing urgency and desperation from 1929 until the catastrophe of 1933. The brilliance and cogency of his works on the German crisis has rarely been equalled, and never excelled, by any marxist.

The central theme of all these writings was the necessity 'For a Workers' United Front Against Fascism', to cite the title of one of the most famous of them. But there was much more than this. Trotsky forced himself to follow in detail the tortuous arguments that Stalin's German acolytes advanced in defence of the indefensible. Thus, his writings of this period take up and refute an extraordinary range of pseudo-marxist argument and, at the same time, expound with exceptional clarity the 'highest expression of proletarian strategy'. Only a very small part of them can be referred to here.

The official press of the Comintern is now depicting the results of the German elections [of September 1930] as a prodigious victory of Communism, which places the slogan of a Soviet Germany on the order of the day. The bureaucratic optimists do not want to reflect on the meaning of the relationship of forces which is disclosed by the election statistics. They examine the figure of Communist votes gained independently of the revolutionary tasks created by the situation and the obstacles it sets up.

The Communist Party received around 4,600,000 votes as against 3,300,000 in 1928. From the standpoint of 'normal' parliamentary machines, the gain of 1,300,000 votes is considerable, even if we take into consideration the rise in the total number of voters. But the gain of the party pales completely beside the leap of fascism from 800,000 to 6,400,000 votes. Of no less significance is the fact that the Social Democracy, in spite of substantial losses, retained its basic cadres and still received a considerably greater number of workers' votes than the Communist Party.

Meanwhile, if we should ask ourselves what combination of international and domestic circumstances could be capable of turning the working class towards Communism with greater velocity, we could not find an example of more favourable circumstances for such a turn than the situation in present day Germany: . . . the economic crisis, the disintegration of the rulers, the crisis of parliamentarianism, the terrific self-exposure of the Social Democracy in power. From the viewpoint of these concrete historical circumstances, the specific gravity of the German Communist Party in the social life of the country, in spite of the gain of 1,300,000 votes, remains proportionately small . . .

In the meantime, the first characteristic of a real revolutionary party is to be able to look reality in the face . . .

For the social crisis to bring about the proletarian revolution, it is necessary that, besides other conditions, a decisive shift of the petty-bourgeois classes occurs in the direction of the proletariat. This will give the proletariat a chance to put itself at the head of the nation as its leader.

The last election revealed - and this is its principal symptomatic significance - a shift in the opposite direction. Under the impact of the crisis, the petty-bourgeoisie swung, not in the direction of the proletarian revolution, but in the direction of the most extreme imperialist reaction, pulling behind it considerable sections of the proletariat.

The gigantic growth of National Socialism is an expression of two factors: a deep social crisis throwing the petty-bourgeois masses off balance, and the lack of a revolutionary party that would today be regarded by the popular masses as the acknowledged revolutionary leader. If the Communist Party is *the party of revolutionary hope*, then fascism, as a mass movement, is *the party of counter-revolutionary despair*. When revolutionary hope embraces the whole proletarian mass, it inevitably pulls behind it on the road of revolution considerable and growing sections of the petty-bourgeoisie. Precisely in this sphere, the election revealed the opposite picture: counter-revolutionary despair embraced the petty-bourgeois mass with such force that it drew behind it many sections of the proletariat . . .

Fascism in Germany has become a real danger, as an acute expression of the helpless position of the bourgeois regime, the conservative role of the Social Democracy in the regime, and the accumulated powerlessness of the Communist Party to abolish it. Whoever denies this is either blind or a braggart.[30]

To mend the situation, Trotsky argued, it was necessary first of all to shake the Communist Party out of its sterile ultra-radicalism. The policy of 'bureaucratic ultimatism' ('an attempt to rape the working class having failed to convince it') must be replaced by one of active manoeuvre grounded in the united front policy.

It is a difficult task to arouse all at once the majority of the German working class for an offensive. As a consequence of the defeats of 1919, 1921 and 1923 and of the adventures of the 'third period' the German workers, who on top of that are bound by powerful conservative organisations, have developed strong centres of inhibition. But, on the other hand, the organisational solidarity of the German workers, which has almost altogether prevented until now the penetration of fascism into their ranks, opens the very greatest possibilities of *defensive* struggles. One must bear in mind that the policy of the united front is in general much more effective for the defensive than for the offensive. The more conservative or backward strata are more easily drawn into a struggle to fight for what they have than for new conquests.[31]

All manner of sophistries were employed by the Stalinists to obscure the issue and to represent what had once been Comintern policy as 'counter-revolutionary Trotskyism'. The united front, it was argued, could come 'only from below', that is, agreements with the social democrats were excluded but individual social democrats could take part in a 'Red United Front' - provided they accepted the leadership of the Communist Party!

And increasingly the fatal illusion - summed up as 'After Hitler, our turn' - was encouraged, a perspective of passivity and impotence masked by radical rhetoric, as Trotsky repeatedly stressed. Again and again he returned to the central issue of the united front, exposing sophistries, brushing aside slanders and thrusting the point home, as in this brilliant example:

> A cattle dealer once drove some bulls to the slaughter house. And the butcher came nigh with his sharp knife.
>
> 'Let us close ranks and jack up this executioner on our horns,' suggested one of the bulls.
>
> 'If you please, in what way is the butcher any worse than the dealer who drove us hither with his cudgel?' replied the bulls, who had received their political education in Manuilsky's institute.
>
> 'But we shall be able to attend to the dealer as well afterwards!'
>
> 'Nothing doing,' replied the bulls, firm in their principles, to the counsellor. 'You are trying to shield our enemies from the left; you are a social-butcher yourself.'
>
> And they refused to close ranks.
>
> - from *Aesop's Fables*[32]

The Communist Party held fast to its fatal course. Hitler came to power. The workers' movement was smashed.

The Popular Front and the Spanish Revolution

Hitler's victory drove the rulers of the USSR to seek 'insurance' by means of a military alliance with the then still dominant Western powers of France and Britain. As an auxiliary to Stalin's diplomacy - for that is what it had now become - the Comintern was jerked hard to the right. The Seventh (and last) Congress was convened in 1935 as a public demonstration that revolution was definitely off the agenda. It called for 'The United People's Front in the struggle for peace and against the instigations of war. All those interested in the preservation of peace should be drawn into this united front'.[33]

Those interested in the preservation of peace included the victors of 1918, the French and British ruling classes, the objects of the new line.

'Today the situation is not what it was in 1914', declared the ECCI in May 1936,

> Now it is not only the working class, the peasantry and all working people who are resolved to maintain peace, but also the oppressed countries and the weak nations whose independence is threatened by war ... In the present phase a number of capitalist states are also concerned to maintain peace. Hence the possibility of creating a broad front of the working class, of all working people and of entire nations against the danger of imperialist war.[34]

Such a 'front' was, of course, necessarily a defence of the imperialist status quo. A reformist rhetoric had to be liberally employed to conceal this fact and was highly successful - for a time.

In the first phase popular enthusiasm for unity brought enormous gains to the Communist Parties - the French Party grew from 30,000 in 1934 to 150,000 by the end of 1936 plus 100,000 in the Communist Youth; the Spanish Party grew from under a thousand at the close of the 'Third Period' (1934) to 35,000 in February 1936 to 117,000 in July 1937. The recruits were armoured against criticism from the left by the belief that the Trotskyists were literally fascist agents.

In May 1935 the Franco-Soviet pact was signed. By July the CP and the French Socialist Party (SFIO) had come to an

72

agreement with the Radical Party, the backbone of French bourgeois democracy, and in April 1936 the 'Front Populaire' of these three parties won a general election on a platform of 'collective security' and reform. The CP gained 72 seats campaigning on the slogan 'For the strong, free and happy France' and became an essential part of the parliamentary majority of Leon Blum, the SFIO leader and Front Populaire Prime Minister. Maurice Thorez, the secretary-general of the PCF, was able to claim: 'We boldly deprived our enemies of the things they had stolen from us and trampled underfoot. We took back the Marseillaise and the Tricolor.'[35]

When the electoral victory of the left was followed by a massive wave of strikes and sit-ins - six million workers were involved in June 1936 - the erstwhile champions of 'ascending revolutionary struggles' exerted themselves to contain the movement within narrow limits and to end it on the basis of the 'Matignon Agreement' concessions (notably the 40-hour week and holidays with pay). By the end of the year the Communist Party, now to the right of its social-democratic allies, was calling for the extension of the 'Popular Front' into a 'French Front' by the incorporation of some right wing conservatives who were, on nationalist grounds, strongly anti-German.

The French party pioneered these policies because the French alliance was central to Stalin's foreign policy but they were rapidly adopted by the whole Comintern. When the Spanish revolution erupted in July 1936, in response to Franco's attempted seizure of power, the Spanish CP, part of the Spanish Popular Front which had won the February elections and taken power, did its utmost to keep the movement within the framework of 'democracy'. With the aid of Russian diplomacy, and of course the social-democrats, it was successful. 'It is absolutely false', declared Jesus Hernandez, editor of the party's daily paper,

> that the present workers' movement has for its object the establishment of the proletarian dictatorship after the war

has terminated . . . We communists are the first to repudiate this supposition. We are motivated exclusively by a desire to defend the democratic republic.[36]

In pursuit of this line the Spanish Communist Party and its bourgeois allies pushed the policies of the republican government more and more to the right; in the course of the long drawn out civil war, it drove out of the government first the POUM, a party to the left of the CP which Trotsky had bitterly criticised for entering the Popular Front in the first place and so disarming itself politically and providing a 'left' cover for the Communist Party, and then the left wing leaders of the Spanish Socialist Party.

'The defence of republican order while defending property'[37] led to a reign of terror in Republican Spain against the *left*. And this paved the way, Trotsky demonstrated, for Franco's victory.

The Spanish proletariat displayed first-rate military qualities,

he wrote in December 1937

In its specific gravity in the country's economic life, in its political and cultural level, the Spanish proletariat stood on the first day of the revolution not below but above the Russian proletariat at the beginning of 1917. On the road to its victory, its own organisations stood as the chief obstacles. The commanding clique of Stalinists, in accordance with their counter-revolutionary function, consisted of hirelings, careerists, declassed elements, and in general, all types of social refuse. The representatives of other labour organisations - incurable reformists, Anarchist phrasemongers, helpless centrists of the ·POUM - grumbled, groaned, wavered, manoeuvred, but in the end adapted themselves to the Stalinists. As a result of their joint activity, the camp of social revolution - workers and peasants - proved to be subordinated to the bourgeoisie, or more correctly, to its shadow. It was bled white and its character was destroyed.

There was no lack of heroism on the part of the masses or courage on the part of individual revolutionists. But the masses were left to their own resources while the revolutionists remained disunited, without a programme, without a plan of action. The 'republican' military commanders were more concerned with crushing the social revolution than with scoring military victories. The soldiers lost confidence in their commanders, the masses in the government; the peasants stepped aside; the workers became exhausted; defeat followed defeat; demoralisation grew apace. All this was not difficult to foresee from the beginning of the civil war. By setting itself the task of rescuing the capitalist regime, the Popular Front doomed itself to military defeat. By turning Bolshevism on its head, Stalin succeeded completely in fulfilling the role of gravedigger of the revolution.[38]

Scarcely anyone today (apart from a handful of insignificant ex-Maoist sectlets) defends the Stalinist line of the 'Third Period'. The Popular Front is a different matter entirely. Allowing for all the differences of time and place, what else, in essence, is 'Eurocommunism' and the so-called 'historic compromise'? Moreover, some of those well to the left, in formal political terms, of the Eurocommunist trend reproduce the *substance* of the very errors Trotsky fought against under the heading 'Anglo-Soviet Trade Union Committee'.

The issues, then, are not only of historical but also of immediate practical interest. Trotsky's writings on strategy and tactics in relation to these great questions are a veritable treasure house. It can be said without any exaggeration that no one else since 1923 has produced work that even approaches their profundity and brilliance. They are, literally, indispensible to revolutionaries today.

4. Party and Class

Marx affirmed that the emancipation of the working class must be the act of the working class itself; but, he also argued, the ruling classes control the 'means of mental production' and therefore the 'dominant ideas in any epoch are those of the ruling classes'.

From this contradiction arises the necessity for the revolutionary socialist party. The nature of the party and, above all, the nature of its relationship to the working class has been central to socialist movements from the beginning. It has never been merely a 'technical' question of organisation. At each stage the disputes about the relationship of party and class - and therefore about the nature of the party - have also been disputes about the objectives of the movement. The arguments about *means* have always been partly arguments about *ends*, and necessarily so. Thus, Marx's own conflicts with Proudhon, with Schapper, with Blanqui, with Bakunin and many others on this issue were inextricably interwoven with differences about the nature of socialism and the means whereby it was to be achieved.

After Marx's death in 1883, and the death of Engels twelve years later, there was a massive growth of socialist parties. In Russia there soon emerged what was to become a fundamental conflict about the kind of party which had to be built.

Trotsky's first view of the nature of the revolutionary party was essentially that which later came to be regarded as peculiarly 'Leninist'. Indeed, according to Isaac Deutscher,[1] he argued this point of view independently of Lenin while in exile in Siberia in 1901. At any rate he became an early adherent of *Iskra* and at the 1903 Congress of the RSDLP spoke strongly for a highly centralised organisation: 'Our rules . . . represent the organised distrust of the Party towards all its sections, that is, control over all local, district, national and other organisations.'[2]

He recoiled violently from this position after taking the Menshevik side in the split in the *Iskra* tendency at the congress. Within a year Trotsky had become the outstanding critic of Bolshevik centralism; Lenin's methods, he wrote in 1904, 'lead to this: the party organisation is substituted for the party, the Central Committee is substituted for the party organisation, and finally a 'dictator' is substituted for the Central Committee . . . '[3]

Like Rosa Luxemburg, Trotsky was suspicious of 'party conservatism' in general and placed heavy reliance on spontaneous working class action:

> The European socialist parties - and in the first place the mightiest of them, the German - have developed their conservatism which grows stronger in proportion to the size of the masses affected, the efficiency of the organisation, and the party discipline. *Therefore, it is possible that the social democracy may become an obstacle in the path of any open clash between the workers and the bourgoisie.*[4]

To overcome this conservatism, Trotsky relied on the spontaneous sweep of revolution which, he wrote, under the impact of the 1905 revolution, 'kills party routine, destroys party conservatism'. Thus the role of the party is reduced essentially to propaganda. It is not the vanguard of the working class.

There was, of course, considerable justification for his fears. In Russia even the Bolshevik party showed itself to be conservative in 1905-07 and again in 1917.[6] In the West, where conservatism had an incomparably greater *material* basis in the privileges of the labour bureaucracies, it played a decisive counter-revolutionary role in 1918-19.

The experience of 1905, in which Trotsky played a quite extraordinary part as an individual without serious party connections (he was a nominal Menshevik at the time but essentially a freelance), no doubt strengthened his belief in the sufficiency of spontaneous mass action.

In the period of the reaction after 1906, and even in the upturn in the Russian labour movement from 1912, he continued to criticise Bolshevik 'substitutionism' and to preach a 'unity' of all tendencies which was essentially directed *against* the Bolsheviks. Again, this may have contributed to his slowness in recognising the dangers of *real* substitutionism after 1920.

Trotsky's position of 1904-17 was shown to be clearly untenable by the course of events. Without Lenin, Trotsky later wrote, there would have been no October revolution. But it was not simply a question of Lenin arriving at the Finland Station in April 1917. It was a matter of the party which Lenin and his collaborators had built over the previous years. The conservatism of many of the leaders of that party (reinforced, it must be said, by the theoretical scheme of the 'democratic dictatorship' which Lenin had defended for so long) would very probably have prevented the seizure of power but for Lenin's unique authority and determination. Without the party, with all its defects, the question could not even arise. 'Spontaneous' mass action can sometimes bring down an authoritarian regime. It did so in Russia in February 1917, in Germany and in Austria-Hungary in 1918, and has done so on various occasions since, most recently in Iran.

In 1917 Trotsky adopted the view that for the workers to take and hold power, a party of Lenin's type was indispensible. He never subsequently wavered from it and indeed gave it characteristically sharp expression. In 1932 in rebutting the argument that 'the interests of the class come before the interests of the party' he wrote:

The class, taken by itself, is only material for exploitation.

The proletariat assumes an independent role only at the moment when from a social class *in itself* it becomes a political class *for itself*. This cannot take place otherwise than through the medium of a party. The party is that historical organ by means of which the class becomes class conscious. To say that 'the class stands higher than the party' is to assert that the class in the raw stands higher than the class which is on the road to class consciousness. Not only is this incorrect: it is reactionary.[7]

This conception presents some very obvious difficulties. In particular, experience had shown that the 'historical organ' through which a particular working class achieved consciousness could degenerate. How then can party organisation be defended?

The Historically Conditioned Instrument

Trotsky was well aware of this problem. He had witnessed the disintegration of the International in 1914, the *directly* counter-revolutionary role of social democracy in 1918-19 and, of course, the rise of Stalinism.

The passage quoted above continues:

The progress of a class towards class consciousness, that is, the building of a revolutionary party which leads the proletariat, is a complex and a contradictory process. The class itself is not homogeneous. Its different sections arrive at class consciousness by different paths and at different times. The bourgeoisie participates actively in this process. Within the working class it creates its own institutions, or utilises those already existing, in order to oppose certain strata of workers against others. Within the proletariat several parties are active at the same time. Therefore, for the greater part of its political journey, it remains split politically. The problem of the united front - which arises during certain periods most sharply - originates therein. The historical interests of the proletariat find their expression in the Communist Party - when its policies are correct. The task of the Communist Party consists of winning over the majority of the proletariat; and only thus is the socialist revolution made possible. The Communist Party cannot fulfil its mission except by preserving, completely and unconditionally, its political and organisational independence apart from all other parties and organisations within and without the working class. To transgress this basic principle of marxist policy is to commit the most heinous of crimes against the interests of the proletariat as a class ... But the proletariat moves towards revolutionary consciousness not by passing grades in school but by passing through the class struggle, which abhors interruptions. To fight, the proletariat must have unity in its ranks. This holds true for partial economic conflicts within the walls of a single factory as well as such 'national' political battles as the one to repel fascism. Consequently the tactic of the united front is not something accidental and artificial - a cunning manoeuvre - not at all; it originates entirely and wholly, in the objective conditions governing the development of the proletariat.[8]

This remarkably clear, coherent and realistic analysis was not, of course, a timeless sociological generalisation. It was rooted in actual historical development. The parties of the Second International had, in their time, helped to create those:

bulwarks of workers' democracy [the workers' organisations, especially the unions] within the bourgeois state ... [which] are absolutely essential for taking the revolutionary road. The work of the Second International consisted in creating just such bulwarks during the epoch when it was still fulfilling its progressive historic labour.[9]

The parties of that International were in time rotted from

within by adaptation to the societies in which they operated; this development had, of course, a material and not merely an ideological basis. Faced with the test of 4 August 1914, they capitulated to 'their own' bourgeoisie (with certain exceptions: the Bolsheviks, the Bulgarians, the Serbs) or adopted an equivocal 'centrist' position (the Italians, the Scandinavians, the Americans and various minorities elsewhere). Out of that capitulation, the inner party conflicts and splits that it produced, the rising tide of working class opposition to the war from 1916 onwards and the revolutions of 1917 and 1918, arose the Communist International, 'the direct continuation of the heroic endeavours and martyrdom of a long line of revolutionary generations from Babeuf to Karl Liebknecht and Rosa Luxemburg'.[10]

This was now the 'historic organ by means of which the class becomes class conscious'. The parties of the Communist International had, especially since 1923 committed a series of blunders (Trotsky was not, of course, blind to their earlier mistakes), and increasingly followed opportunist or sectarian policies under the direction of Stalin and his ruling circle in the USSR. Nevertheless, with all its defects it was a *reality*, not a hypothesis; a reality which commanded the support or sympathy of millions around the world. Indeed, paradoxically, its very defects indicated in a distorted way that it was a truly mass organisation. For Trotsky did not subscribe to the simplistic view that the big parties of the Comintern were *merely* instruments of the Stalinist bureaucracy in Russia. The problem was to correct their course. 'All eyes to the Communist Party. We must explain to it. We must convince it.'[11]

As a matter of political necessity, the party's internal regime must be democratic:

> The internal struggle trains the party and makes its own road clear to it. In this struggle all the members of the party gain a deep confidence in the correctness of the policy of the party and in the revolutionary reliability of

the leadership. Only such a conviction in the rank and file Bolshevik, won through experience and ideological struggle, gives the leadership the chance to lead the whole party into battle at the necessary moment. And only a deep confidence of the party itself in the correctness of its policy inspires the working masses with confidence in the party. Artificial splits forced from the outside; the absence of a free and honest ideological struggle...this is what now paralyses the Spanish Communist Party,[12]

Trotsky wrote in 1931. The argument applied generally.

It was, however, not so simple. Soon after his expulsion from the USSR in 1929 Trotsky outlined what he considered to be the basic questions for supporters of the Left Opposition in Europe (attitudes to the Anglo-Russian Trade Union Committee, the Chinese Revolution and to 'Socialism in One Country').

Some comrades may be astonished that I omit reference here to the question of the party regime,

he continued,

I do so not out of oversight but deliberately. A party regime has no independent, self-sufficient meaning. In relation to party policy it is a derivative magnitude. The most heterogeneous elements sympathise with the struggle against Stalinist bureaucratism... For a Marxist, democracy within a party or within a country is not an abstraction. Democracy is always conditioned by the struggle of living forces. By bureaucratism, the opportunist elements ... understand revolutionary centralism. Obviously, they cannot be our co-thinkers.[13]

It is possible to go through Trotsky's post-1917 writings, and even his writings after 1929 or 1934, and to produce a series of statements, some exalting the virtues of inner-party democracy and condemning 'administrative' measures against critics, others arguing the necessity for purges and expulsions. Nor is it a case of quotations wrenched from their context. For Trotsky, the relationship between centralism and inner-party democracy was not constant. It was a question of the *political content* of each in specific but changing circumstances. Trotsky wrote towards the end of 1932:

> The principle of party democracy is in no way identical with the principle of the open door. The Left Opposition has never demanded of the Stalinists that they transform the party into a mechanical sum of factions, groups, sects and individuals. We accuse the centrist bureaucracy of carrying on an essentially false policy which at every step brings them into contradiction with the flower of the proletariat and of looking for the way out of these contradictions by the strangling of party democracy.[14]

This may appear equivocal. Indeed, in purely formal terms it *is* equivocal. The solution to the contradiction is to be found in the dynamics of party development. The party, Trotsky believed, cannot grow, in terms of real mass influence as opposed to mere numbers, except through a reciprocal relationship, a process of interaction, with wider and wider layers of workers. For *this* inner-party democracy is indispensable. It provides the means of feedback of class experience into the party. Such a development is not always possible. Often, objective circumstances rule out such growth. But the party must always be attuned to the possibility. Otherwise it will not be able to seize the chances that occur from time to time.

Therefore, the regime must *at all times* be as open and flexible as possible, consonant with preserving the revolutionary integrity of the party. The qualification is important. For unfavourable circumstances weaken the ties between the party and the layers of advanced workers and so increase the problem of 'factions, groups, sects' which can become an *obstacle* to the growth of inner-party democracy understood as Trotsky understood it, essentially a mechanism by which the party relates to wider sections of the working class, learning from them and at the same time earning the right to lead them.

The argument is, perhaps, too abstract. To concretise it, consider this passage from Trotsky's *History of the Russian Revolution*, discussing Lenin's isolation from the majority of the party leadership after the February revolution.

> Against the old Bolsheviks [in April 1917] Lenin found support in another layer of the party, already tempered, but more fresh and more closely united with the masses. In the February revolution, as we know, the worker-Bolsheviks played the decisive role. They thought it self-evident that the class which had won the victory should seize power ... Almost everywhere there were left Bolsheviks accused of maximalism, even of anarchism. These worker-revolutionists only lacked the theoretical resources to defend their position. But they were ready to respond to the first clear call. It was on this stratum of workers, decisively risen to their feet during the upward years of 1912-14, that Lenin was now banking.[15]

That model appears again and again in Trotsky's writings. A mass party, unlike a sect, is necessarily buffeted by immensely powerful forces, especially in revolutionary circumstances. These forces inevitably find expression inside the party also. To keep the party on course (in practice, to continually correct its course in a changing situation) the complex relationship between the leadership, the various layers of the cadre and the workers they influence and are influenced by, expresses itself and *must* express itself in political struggle inside the party. If that is artificially smothered by administrative means, the party will lose its way.

An indispensable function of the leadership, itself formed by selection in previous struggles, is to understand when to close ranks to preserve the core of the organisation from disintegration by unfavourable outside pressures - to emphasise centralism - and when to open up the organisation and to use layers of advanced workers inside *and outside* the party to overcome the party conservatism of sections of the cadre and leadership - to emphasise democracy - in order to change course quickly.

All of this implies a very exalted conception of the role of leadership, and this the post-1917 Trotsky certainly had. He was to affirm in 1938 that 'The historical crisis of mankind is reduced to the crisis of revolutionary leadership.' It was a conception, however, of the organic growth of a leading cadre in relation to the experiences of the party in the actual class struggle. Of course, the leading cadre had to embody a tradition and the experience of the past (from Babeuf to Karl Liebknecht), a knowledge of the strategy and tactics that had been tested in many countries at different times over many years. This knowledge was necessarily, for the most part, theoretical and Trotsky least of all was inclined to under-value it. It was a necessary condition for successful leadership but not a sufficient one. The experience of the party in action and of its changing relationship to various sections of workers was the additional, irreplaceable factor which could be developed only in practice.

An Anomaly

In Trotsky's lifetime only one Communist Party, that in the USSR, held state power (other than in the areas controlled by the Chinese Communist Party in the thirties).

Trotsky classed them all as 'bureaucratic centrist' organisations, that is to say workers' organisations which vacillated between revolutionary and reformist politics. After 1935, with the Popular Front line, he concluded that they had become social-patriotic; 'yellow agencies of rotting capitalism'.[16]

But these terms refer to workers' organisations; to parties which are obliged to compete with other parties for support in their own working class movements. The CPSU, certainly after 1929 if not earlier, was not a party at all in that sense. It was a bureaucratic apparatus, the instrument of a totalitarian despotism. Trotsky conceded this in part: 'The party [that is, the CPSU] as a party does not exist today. The centrist apparatus has strangled it',[17] he wrote in 1930. But he did conclude that the CPSU was a *fundamentally* different species from the workers' parties outside the USSR.

Even after he had abandoned hope (in October 1933) of a peaceful reform of the regime in the USSR the confusion remained. Of course it was associated with the belief that even though reform was impossible, the USSR nonetheless remained a degenerated workers' state.

The matter became important a few years after Trotsky's death when a series of new Stalinist states came into being without proletarian revolutions and with a series of ruling 'Communist Parties' which manifestly were not workers' parties in terms of Trotsky's conception. The contradiction was already built into Trotsky's own post-1933 position.

The Thread is Cut

We have seen that Trotsky's mature conception of the relationship between party and class was neither abstract nor arbitrary, but was rooted *both* in the experience of Bolshevism in Russia and in the actual historical development which had led to mass Communist Parties in a number of important countries.

But what if that development runs into the sands? What if the 'historically conditioned instrument' fails the test? Trotsky had contemplated the possibility, only to reject it firmly. In 1931 he wrote:

> Let us take another, more remote example for the clarification of our ideas. Hugo Urbahns, who considers himself a 'Left Communist', declares the German party bankrupt, politically done for, and proposes to create a new party. If Urbahns were right, it would mean that the

victory of fascism is certain. For, in order to create a new party, years are required (and there has been nothing to prove that the party of Urbahns would in any sense be better than Thaelmann's party: when Urbahns was at the head of the party, there were by no means fewer mistakes). Yes, should the fascists really conquer power, that would mean not only the physical destruction of the Communist Party, but veritable political bankruptcy for it...The seizure of power by the fascists would therefore most probably signify the necessity of creating a new revolutionary party and in all likelihood also a new International. That would be a frightful historical catastrophe. But to assume today that all this is *unavoidable* can be done only by genuine liquidators, those who under the mantle of hollow phrases are really hastening to capitulate like cravens in the face of the struggle and *without* a struggle ... We are unshakably convinced that the victory over the fascists is possible - not after their coming to power, not after five, ten or twenty years of their rule, but now, under the given conditions, in the coming months and weeks.[18]

But Hitler did come to power. Notwithstanding the brilliance and cogency of Trotsky's arguments the German Communist Party, with its quarter of a million members and its six million votes (in 1932), held fast to its fatal course. It was smashed, without resistance, along with the 'social fascists', the trade unions and each and every one of the political, cultural and social organisations created by the German working class in the previous sixty years.

In 1931 Trotsky had described Germany as 'the key to the international situation...On the development in which the solution of the German crisis occurs will depend not only the fate of Germany itself (and that is already a great deal) but the fate of Europe, the destiny of the entire world, for many years to come.'[19]

It was an accurate forecast. The defeat of the German

working class transformed *world* politics. The failure of the Communist Party even to attempt resistance was a blow as heavy as the capitulation of social democracy had been in 1914. It was the 4th of August of the Communist International.

What then is left of the 'historic organ by means of which the class becomes class conscious'? From 1933 until his death in August 1940 Trotsky wrestled with what proved to be an insoluble dilemma, at that time and long afterwards. In June 1932 he had written:

> The Stalinists by their persecution would like to push us on the road of a second party and a fourth international. They understand that a fatal error of this type on the part of the Opposition would slow up its growth for years, if not nullify all its successes altogether.[20]

Now, less than a year later he was forced to concede, first, that the German party was finished, then a little later (after the Comintern executive declared in April 1933 that its policy in Germany was 'completely correct') that *all* the Communist Parties were finished as revolutionary organisations, that what was needed were 'New Communist Parties and the New International' (the title of an article dated July 1933).

The connecting rod between theory and practice had been cut. Before 1917 Trotsky had relied on spontaneous working class action to overcome party conservatism. After 1917 he recognised the revolutionary workers' *party* as the *indispensible* instrument of socialist revolution. The lack of such parties rooted in the working class, and possessing mature, experienced cadres, had produced the tragedy of 1918-19 - mass revolutionary movements in Germany, Austria, Hungary and, elsewhere, mass spontaneous struggles - leading to defeat.

The means of overcoming the defect - the parties of the Communist International - had themselves degenerated to the point where they had become obstacles to a revolutionary solution of new profound social crises.

It was necessary to start again. But what was left to start

with? Essentially there was nothing but small (often tiny) groups, whose common characteristics included isolation from the actual workers' movements and from direct involvement in workers' struggles. The apparent partial exceptions to this generalisation - those who could count their members in hundreds or thousands rather than dozens - the Greek Archiomarxists, the Dutch RSAP and, a little later, the Spanish POUM, all proved to be frail reeds; centrists rather than revolutionaries, obstacles rather than allies.

With such forces Trotsky began to reconstruct. He had no choice, unless retreat into passivity or that disguised passivity later called 'Western marxism' are reckoned as choices. But means and ends are inextricably interwoven. With the links to the real workers' movement cut, 'Trotskyism', even in Trotsky's lifetime, began to accommodate to its actual milieu - small radicalised sections of the intellectual strata of the petty bourgeoisie. As we shall see, Trotsky himself fought a long battle against this accommodation. At the same time, the cruel necessities of the situation drove him to adopt positions which, in spite of his will and understanding, assisted in its growth.

The New International

If the Communist Left throughout the world consisted of only five individuals, they would nevertheless have been obliged to build an international organisation *simultaneously* with the building of one or more national organisations. It is wrong to view a national organisation as the foundation and the International as a roof. The interrelation here is of an entirely different type. Marx and Engels started the communist movement with an international document in 1847 and with the creation of an international movement. The same thing was repeated in the creation of the First International. The same path was followed by the Zimmerwald Left in preparation for the Third International. Today this road is dictated far more imperiously than in the days of Marx. It is, of course, possible in the epoch of imperialism for a revolutionary proletarian tendency to arise in one or another country, but it cannot thrive and develop in one isolated country; on the very next day after its formation it must seek or create international ties, an international platform, because a guarantee of the correctness of the national policy can be found only along this road. A tendency which remains shut in nationally over a stretch of years condemns itself irrevocably to degeneration.[21]

Trotsky wrote this, in a polemic with Bordiga's Italian ultra-left sect, while he (Trotsky) was still committed to a policy of reform of the existing Communist Parties. He was arguing for an international faction orienting on an existing International. The logic of that position, as opposed to the arguments used to sustain it, seemed irrefutable.

The *arguments* themselves will not withstand critical examination. Marx and Engels did not start with the 'creation of an international movement'. The Communist Manifesto was written for an already *existing* Communist League (albeit of very primitive communist ideas) which was international only in the sense that it existed in several countries. It was essentially a *German* organisation, consisting of German emigre artisans and intellectuals in Paris, Brussels and elsewhere, as well as groups in the Rhineland and German Switzerland.

The First International started as an alliance between existing British trade union organisations under liberal influence and existing French ones under Proudhonist influence, and later drew in other groupings of very diverse character and nationality. Far from 'repeating' the experience of the Communist League, it was developed on exactly the *opposite* lines - without an initial programmatic basis and without a centralised organisation. The same is true, to a much lesser degree, of the Second International, which Trotsky does not mention here.

Nor will the reference to the Zimmerwald Left stand

either. The Zimmerwald *Left* (as opposed to the Zimmerwald current as a whole) consisted of the Bolshevik Party, a mass national party, plus more or less isolated individuals ('one Lithuanian, the Pole Karl Radek, two Swedish delegates and Julian Borchard, the delegate of a tiny group, the German International Socialists.')[22]

Practically speaking, Trotsky had no option. He had no base in any workers' movement now. All contact with his supporters in the USSR had ceased by the spring of 1933.[23] It was a matter of pulling together whatever could be pulled together, wherever it existed, to create a political current. Moreover the argument that an international platform was needed - or a common analysis of the problems of the working class movement - was indisputable. Trotsky supplied it. But a confusion between ideas and organisation, between political tendency and international *party*, had been introduced. Within a few years, Trotsky tacitly abandoned his conception of the revolutionary party as the 'historical organ by means of which the class becomes class conscious' and launched an 'International' without a significant base in *any* workers' movement.

First, however, Trotsky attempted to find new forces. The Trotskyist groups were tiny. The power of the Stalinists had forced them into a political ghetto. This, moreover, had a definite social location in a section of the petty-bourgeois intelligentsia.

How to break out, proletarianise Trotskyism and pull significant numbers of workers into new communist parties?

There were enormous obstacles in the way. A major long term effect of the defeat in Germany was to create such a massive groundswell for unity amongst working class militants that the call for new parties and a new International, in other words for a new split, fell on the stoniest of ground. Trotsky had pioneered the call for the workers' united front against fascism. But as this call began to gain ground in the Socialist parties after 1933 (and, soon, in the Communist parties too) Trotsky's followers could be and were represented as splitters;

they were now calling for new parties and a new International. Their isolation was reinforced.

After initial attempts to 'regroup' with various centrist and left-reformist groups (for example, the British ILP) had foundered (producing a rich crop of polemics against centrism from Trotsky), Trotsky proposed the drastic step of entry into the social-democratic parties. Strictly speaking, this was argued for specific cases - France at first (hence the term 'French Turn') - but it came to be generalised in practice. The arguments were that the social democrats were moving to the left, so creating a more favourable climate for revolutionary work; that they were attracting new layers of workers and presented an incomparably more proletarian environment than the isolated propaganda groups which Trotskyism inhabited.

The operation was conceived of as short-term; a sharp, hard fight with the reformists and centrists, then a split and the founding of the party. 'Entry into a reformist or centrist party in itself does not include a long-term perspective. It is only a stage which under certain conditions can be limited to an episode.'[24]

In the event the operation failed in its strategic aim; it failed to change the relationship of forces or to improve the social composition of the Trotskyist grouplets. The fundamental reasons for the failure were the consequences of the defeat in Germany and the turning of the Communist International, first to the United Front (1934) and then to the Popular Front (1935), the great impact these changes made and the consequent swing rightwards of the whole workers' movement. In addition Stalin's anti-Trotsky campaign soon had Trotsky and his followers denounced as fascist agents.

The circumstances which had made it possible for revolutionaries to win *mass* leftwards-moving centrist parties like the German USPD and the majority of French Socialists to the Communist International in 1919-21 simply did not exist in 1934-35. Whatever mistakes Trotsky or his followers may have made in the course of the 'French Turn' can have had only trivial effects by comparison with the effects of the profoundly unfavourable situation.

Some of the gains claimed from the entry tactic were real. It involved a break with many whom Trotsky called 'conservative sectarians', that is those who could not adjust to active politics, as opposed to small circle propagandism in the intellectual milieu.

Towards the end of 1933 Trotsky wrote:

> A revolutionary organisation cannot develop without purging itself, especially under conditions of legal work, when not infrequently chance, alien and degenerate elements gather under the banner of revolution...We are making an important revolutionary turn. At such moments inner crisis or splits are absolutely inevitable. To fear them is to substitute petty-bourgeois sentimentalism and personal scheming for revolutionary policy. The League [the French Trotskyist group] is passing through a first crisis under the banner of great and clear revolutionary criteria. Under these conditions a splitting off of a part of the League will be a great step forward. It will reject all that is unhealthy, crippled and incapacitated; it will give a lesson to the vacillating and irresolute elements; it will harden the better sections of the youth; it will improve the inner atmosphere; it will open up before the League new, great possibilities.[25]

No doubt all this was correct in principle and, in fact, some new forces were recruited from the socialist youth organisations to replace those who were eliminated (or rather, dropped out in most cases). Nevertheless, the balance of forces - the pathetic weakness of the revolutionary left - remained basically unaltered. What then?

Trotsky pressed on with the foundation of the Fourth International. After repeatedly stating that it could not be an *immediate* perspective, as the forces were not yet available - as late as 1935 he had denounced as 'a stupid piece of gossip' the idea that 'the Trotskyists want to proclaim the Fourth International next Thursday' - he proposed, within a year, precisely that: the proclamation of the New International. On that occasion he was unable to persuade his followers. By 1938 he had won them over.

The forces adhering to the Fourth International in 1938 were weaker, not stronger, than those which had existed in 1934. (The SWP of the USA was the only serious exception). The Spanish revolution had been strangled in the meantime. Trotsky justified his decision by a partial and unacknowledged retreat into the semi-spontaneity he had advocated before 1917, and also by analogy with Lenin's position in 1914.

> The discrepancy between our forces and the tasks on the morrow is much more clearly perceived by us than by our critics,

wrote Trotsky in late 1938.

> But the harsh and tragic dialectic of our epoch is working in our favour. Brought to the extreme pitch of exasperation and indignation, the masses will find no other leadership than that offered by the Fourth International.[27]

But 1917 had shown positively, and 1918-19 negatively and, above all, 1936 in Spain had demonstrated the indispensibility of parties rooted in their national working classes through a long period of struggle for partial demands. Trotsky had recognised this more clearly than most. Now, since such parties did not exist, and the need was extraordinarily urgent, he took refuge in a 'Weltgeist' of revolution that would somehow create them out of spontaneous 'exasperation and indignation' provided 'a spotless banner' were waved aloft. The spontaneous upsurge would, in the course of the war or soon after, lift the isolated and inexperienced 'leaderships' of the Fourth International sections into leadership of mass parties.

The analogy with Lenin in 1914 was doubly inappropriate. When Lenin wrote in 1914: 'The Second International is dead:

94

Long live the Third International', he was already the most influential leader of a real mass party in a major country. Nevertheless, he did not think of calling for the founding of the Third International until one and a half years after the October revolution and at a time when, he believed, a mass and ascending revolutionary movement existed in Europe. That Trotsky should ignore all this was a tribute to his revolutionary will. Politically, however, this would derail and disorient his followers when, after his death, a very real upsurge passed them by - as was inevitable given their isolation - and would make it much harder for them to develop a realistic revolutionary orientation.

There was an element of near-messianism in Trotsky's conceptions at this time. In a desperately difficult situation, with fascism in the ascendant, defeat piled on defeat for the workers' movement and a new world war imminent, the banner of revolution had to be flown, the programme of communism reasserted, until the revolution itself transformed the situation.

Perhaps it would have been impossible to hold his followers together without something of this outlook which, if so, was therefore a *necessary* deviation from his mature view. But its later costs were none the less real.

5. The Heritage

The essence of tragedy, Trotsky once wrote, is the contrast between great ends and insignificant means. Whatever is to be said about this as a generalisation, it certainly epitomises Trotsky's own plight in the last years of his life. The man who had actually organised the October insurrection, who had directed the operations of the red armies, who had dealt with - as friend or foe - the mass workers' parties (revolutionary and reformist) through the Comintern, was now reduced to struggling to hold together a scatter of tiny groups, virtually all of them impotent to affect the course of events, even marginally.

He was forced to intervene again and again in a hundred petty squabbles in a score of little grouplets. Some of the disputes did, of course, involve serious issues of political principle, but even these, as Trotsky himself saw clearly, were largely rooted in the isolation of the groups from the actual working class movement and the influence of their petty-bourgeois milieu - because that was the milieu into which they had been driven and to which so many of them adapted.

Nevertheless he fought on to the end. Inevitably, his enforced isolation from effective participation in the workers' movement, in which he had once played so big a part, affected to some extent his understanding of the ever-changing course of the class struggle. Not even his vast experience and superb tactical reflexes could substitute entirely for the lack of feedback from the militants engaged in the day to day struggle that is possible only in a real communist party. As the period of isolation lengthened, this became more apparent. Compare his 'Transitional Programme' of 1938 with its prototype, the

'Programme of Action' for France (1934). In freshness, relevance, specificity and concreteness in relation to an actual struggle, the latter is clearly superior.

This was certainly not a question of any failing of intellectual power. Some of Trotsky's last unfinished writings, notably *Trade Unions in the Epoch of Imperialist Decay*, are path-breaking contributions to marxist thought. It is a matter of lack of intimate contact with significant numbers of militants engaged in actual class struggle.

Yet when Trotsky was murdered in August 1940 by Stalin's agent Jacson-Mercader he did leave behind him a *movement*. Whatever the frailties and failings of that movement, and they were manifold, it was a tremendous achievement. The growth of Stalinism, and then the triumph of fascism in most of Europe, nearly obliterated the authentic communist tradition in the workers' movement. Fascism destroyed directly. It smashed the workers' organisations wherever it came to power. Stalinism did the same thing by different means inside the USSR. Outside the USSR it corrupted and then effectively strangled the revolutionary tradition as a *mass* movement.

It is difficult today to appreciate the full force of the torrent of slander and vilification to which Trotsky and his followers were subjected in the thirties. The entire propaganda resources of the USSR and of the Comintern parties were devoted to denouncing 'Trotskyites' (both genuine and spurious) as agents of Hitler, the Japanese Emperor and every kind of reaction. The slaughter of the old Bolsheviks in the USSR (some after spectacular 'show trials', most by murder without the pretext of a trial) was represented as a triumph for the forces of 'socialism and peace', as the Stalinist slogan of the time went.

> Every weak, corrupt or ambitious traitor to Socialism within the Soviet Union has been hired to do the foul work of capitalism and fascism,

declared the Report of the CC to the 15th Congress of the Communist Party of Great Britain in 1938.

> In the forefront of all the wrecking, sabotage and assassination is the fascist agent Trotsky. But the defences of the Soviet people are strong. Under the leadership of our Bolshevik Comrade Yezhov, the spies and wreckers have been exposed before the world and brought to judgement.[1]

Yezhov, who rose to power on the judicial murder of his predecessor Yagoda, was the police chief who presided over the slaughter of communists and many, many others in the USSR in 1937-38, at the height of the Stalinist terror.

The official line, pronounced by Stalin himself, was that 'Trotskyism is the spearhead of the counter-revolutionary bourgeoisie, waging the struggle against communism.' [2] This massive campaign of lies, assisted by the numerous 'liberal' and social-democratic fellow-travellers who were attracted to the CPs after 1935, was kept up for more than twenty years. It served to inoculate CP militants against marxist criticism of Stalinism. Of at least equal importance for small revolutionary organisations of the time, was the general demoralisation engendered by the collapse of the Popular Fronts and the approach of the second world war.

Trotsky expressed it vividly in a discussion in the spring of 1939.

> We are not progressing politically. Yes, it is a fact, which is an expression of a general decay of the workers' movement in the last fifteen years. It is the more general cause. When the revolutionary movement in general is declining, when one defeat follows another, when fascism is spreading over the world, when the official 'marxism' is the most powerful organisation of the deception of the workers, and so on, it is an inevitable situation that the revolutionary elements must work against the general historic

current, even if our ideas, our explanations, are as exact and wise as one can demand. But the masses are not educated by prognostic conception, but by general experiences of their lives. It is the most general explanation - the whole situation is against us.[3]

The little Fourth Internationalist movement that survived these glacial conditions under Trotsky's inspiration and guidance, was politically scarred by the experience to a greater degree than was immediately apparent. It was subsequently to undergo further mutations. Nevertheless, it was the *only* genuinely communist current of any significance to survive the ice age.

World Outlook 1938-40
At the core of Trotsky's view of the world in his last years was the conviction that the capitalist system was near its last gasp.

The economic prerequisite for the proletarian revolution has already in general achieved the highest point of fruition that can be reached under capitalism. Mankind's productive forces stagnate. Already, new inventions and improvements fail to raise the level of material wealth,

he wrote in his 1938 Programme.

Conjunctural crises under the conditions of the social crisis of the whole capitalist system inflict ever heavier deprivations and sufferings upon the masses. Growing unemployment, in its turn, deepens the financial crisis of the state and undermines the unstable monetary systems. Democratic regimes, as well as fascist, stagger from one crisis to another.[4]

As it stands, that could pass as a description of the state of most of the world economy at the time. As has been said,

Trotsky was profoundly impressed by the contrast between this stagnation and the rapid industrial growth of the USSR (there were other important exceptions too, which Trotsky did not consider: industrial output in Japan *doubled* between 1927 and 1936 and went on growing, and in Hitler's Germany unemployment virtually disappeared in the drive for rearmament).

But Trotsky was engaged in more than description. He believed that the situation for capitalism was irretrievable. 'The disintegration of capitalism has reached extreme limits, likewise the disintegration of the old ruling class. The further existence of this system is impossible',[5] he wrote in 1939.

That being so, the reformist workers' parties could not make any gains for their supporters, 'when every serious demand of the proletariat and even every serious demand of the petty bourgeoisie inevitably reaches beyond the limits of capitalist property relations and of the bourgeois state,'[6] as the 1938 Programme put it.

That did not mean that the mass parties of reformism would automatically disappear - historical inertia and the lack of an *obvious* alternative would preserve them for a little while. But they no longer had any relatively secure basis. They had been destabilised. The shock of war and the post-war crisis would wreck them.

These parties, Trotsky believed, included the communist parties.

The definite passing over of the Comintern to the side of the bourgeois order, its cynically counter-revolutionary role throughout the world, particularly in Spain, France, the United States and other 'democratic countries', created exceptional supplementary difficulties for the world proletariat. Under the banner of the October Revolution, the conciliatory policies practised by the 'People's Front' dooms the working class to impotence.[7]

He had held, since 1935, that 'Nothing now distinguishes the Communists from the Social Democrats except the

100

traditional phraseology, which is not difficult to unlearn.'[8]

The reality was to prove more complex, a fact which eventually precipitated a fundamental crisis in the Fourth Internationalist movement. Trotsky was pointing to a real trend, but the time scale for its development was very much greater than he thought. After the Hitler-Stalin Pact (August 1939) the Comintern parties stayed loyal to Moscow and in the 'cold war' from late 1948 onwards they did not capitulate to 'their own' bourgeoisies either. Their policies were not revolutionary but neither were they simply reformist in the ordinary sense. They retained, for nearly twenty years, a 'leftist' orientation to the bourgeois state (consolidated by their systematic exclusion from office in France, Italy and elsewhere after 1947) which made the creation of a revolutionary alternative extremely difficult, even if other factors had been more favourable.

And in one great case, China, and some lesser ones (amongst them Albania, Yugoslavia and North Vietnam) Stalinist parties actually destroyed weak bourgeois states and replaced them by regimes on the Russian pattern. In particular, the Chinese revolution of 1948-49 put the classic Trotskyist analysis of the Stalinist parties into question, at any rate for the backward countries. For if it was regarded as a proletarian revolution, the basis of the Fourth International's existence - the essentially counter-revolutionary nature of Stalinism - was destroyed. If, on the other hand, it was, in some sense, a bourgeois revolution - a 'New Democracy' as Mao Tse-tung claimed at the time - the theory of Permanent Revolution was undermined. This aspect of the matter will be considered later. What is relevant here is that the occurrence of the revolution, whatever view was taken of its nature, refurbished the revolutionary image of Stalinism for a long time.

But the most important mistake Trotsky made at this time was to assume that capitalism had no way out economically, even if the proletarian revolution was averted. That this *was* his belief is indisputable. 'If, however, it is conceded,' he wrote towards the end of 1939, that the present war will provoke not revolution but a decline of the proletariat, then there remains another alternative: the further decay of monopoly capitalism, its further fusion with the state and the replacement of democracy wherever it still remained by a totalitarian regime. The inability of the proletariat to take into its hands the leadership of society could actually lead under these conditions to the growth of a new exploiting class from the Bonapartist fascist bureaucracy. This would be, according to all indications, a regime of decline, signalling the eclipse of civilisation.[9]

Trotsky might, if pressed, have conceded that some temporary economic revival was possible on a cyclical basis. He had been quick to note the limited revival of European capitalism in 1920-21 (and to draw political conclusions from it) and had pointed out a certain revival from the depths of 1929-31 in the early thirties. But he completely excluded the possibility of a prolonged upward economic movement such as had given birth to reformism as a mass force in the decades before the first world war.

His was a common view on the left at that time. And yet the evidence was already available that large-scale arms production could produce *overall* economic growth - growth that was not at all limited to the arms sector of the economy. Of course, the evidence related to the direct preparations for the second world war. But suppose preparing for war could be made permanent or semi-permanent?

In fact, after world war two, capitalism experienced a massive revival. Far from economic contraction and decline being dominant, there was an even greater economic expansion than during the 'classic' imperialist phase before 1914. As Michael Kidron pointed out in 1968, 'the system as a whole has never grown as fast for so long as since the War - twice as fast between 1950 and 1964 as between 1913 and 1950 and nearly half as fast again as during the generation before then.'[10]

Reformism got an entirely new lease of life in the developed capitalist countries on the basis of a *rising* standard of living for the mass of the working class. That the massive economic revival, the long boom of the fifties and sixties, was due mainly to greatly increased state expenditure (in particular *arms* expenditure) has been disputed, if rather implausibly, by both reformist and marxist analysts. What cannot be disputed is the *fact* that Trotsky's prognosis was quite wrong. For the political consequences of the boom falsified the prediction that the *immediate* alternatives were *either* proletarian revolution *or* Bonapartist or fascist dictatorship presiding over 'the eclipse of civilisation'. On the contrary, bourgeois democracy and reformist dominance of the workers' movement again became the norm in most of the developed countries.

An indispensible condition for this development was the survival of bourgeois regimes in the great upheavals of 1944-45, when the fascist states were being shattered by the combination of allied military power and a rising tide of popular revolt. In most European countries the social-democratic and communist parties grew rapidly in this critical phase to play a counter-revolutionary role (in eastern as well as western Europe) and the *decisive* counter-revolutionary role in France and Italy.

But Trotsky had taken for granted *both* the revival, in the first stages of revolt, of the established workers' parties (his writings on the Russian revolution alone suffice to establish that beyond dispute) *and* their counter-revolutionary politics. It was because his perspective was one of economic catastrophe, mass pauperisation and the growth of totalitarian statist regimes as the *only* alternative to proletarian revolution *in the short term*, that he believed that this revival of reformism would be very short-lived - a sort of Kerensky interval.

That is why he wrote with such confidence, late in 1938: 'During the next ten years the programme of the Fourth International will become the guide of millions and these revolutionary millions will know how to storm earth and heaven.'[11]

The mood of messianic expectation induced by such statements made sober and realistic assessments of actual shifts in working class consciousness, alterations in the balance of class forces, and tactical changes to gain the maximum advantage from them (the essence of Lenin's political practice) extremely difficult for Trotsky's followers.

Mention must be made here of Trotsky's emphasis on the importance of those 'transitional demands' which gave his 1938 Programme its popular name.

'It is necessary', he wrote,

> to help the masses in the process of daily struggle to find the bridge between present demands and the socialist programme of the revolution. This bridge should include a system of *transitional demands*, stemming from today's conditions and today's consciousness of wide layers of the working class and unalterably leading to one final conclusion: the conquest of power by the proletariat.[12]

Whether or not it is possible to find slogans or 'demands' that meet these exacting specifications depends, very obviously, on circumstances. If at a given time 'today's consciousness of wide layers' is decidedly non-revolutionary, then it will not be transformed by slogans. Changes in actual conditions are needed. The problem at each stage is to find and advance those slogans which not only strike a chord in at least some sections of the working class (ideally, of course, the whole of it) but which are also capable of leading to working class *actions*. Often they will not be transitional in terms of Trotsky's very restricted definition.

Of course Trotsky cannot be held responsible for the tendency of most of his followers to fetishise the notion of transitional demands, and even the specific demands of the 1938 Programme - most obviously the 'sliding scale of wages'. The emphasis he gave to this matter was, however, excessive and encouraged the belief that 'demands' have some value independently of revolutionary organisation in the working class.

The USSR, Stalinism, War and the Outcome

The second world war began with the German attack on Poland which was quickly followed by the partition of the territories of the Polish state between Hitler and Stalin. For nearly two years (from the summer of 1939 to the summer of 1941) Hitler and Stalin were allies, and in that period Stalin's regime was able to annexe the Baltic states, Bessarabia and Bukovina as well as the Western Ukraine and Western Byelorussia.

From 1935 until then, Stalin's foreign policy had been directed towards achieving a military alliance with France and Britain against Hitler. The Popular Front policy of the Comintern was its counterpart. With the Hitler-Stalin pact, the Communist parties swung round to an 'anti-war' position, the actual content of which was anything but revolutionary, until Hitler's attack on the USSR (after which they became superpatriotic in the 'allied' countries).

The Hitler-Stalin pact and the partition of Poland produced a revulsion against the USSR in left circles outside the Communist parties (and a fair number of desertions from them too) which had its impact on Trotskyist groups also. In the biggest of them, the American Socialist Workers' Party, an opposition began to question Trotsky's slogan 'unconditional defence of the USSR against imperialism', which followed from his definition of the USSR as a 'degenerated workers' state', and, soon, that definition itself.

In the course of the dispute that followed Trotsky gave his analysis of Stalinism in the USSR its final development and considered - in order to reject - alternative positions.

> Let us begin by posing the question of the nature of the Soviet state not on the abstract sociological plane but on the plane of concrete political tasks,

he wrote in September 1939.

> Let us concede for the moment that the bureaucracy is a

new 'class' and that the present regime in the USSR is a special system of class exploitation. What new political conclusions follow for us from these definitions? The Fourth International long ago recognised the necessity of overthrowing the bureaucracy by means of a revolutionary uprising of the toilers. Nothing else is proposed or can be proposed by those who proclaim the bureaucracy to be an exploiting 'class'. The goal to be attained by the overthrow of the bureaucracy is the re-establishment of the rule of the Soviets, expelling from them the present bureaucracy. Nothing different can be proposed or is proposed by the leftist critics. It is the task of the regenerated soviets to collaborate with the world revolution and the building of a socialist society. The overthrow of the bureaucracy therefore presupposes the preservation of state property and of the planned economy ... inasmuch as the question of overthrowing the parasitic oligarchy still remains linked with that of preserving the nationalised (state) property, we call the future revolution *political*. Certain of our critics (Ciliga, Bruno and others) want, come what may, to call the future revolutions *social*. Let us grant this definition. What does it alter in essence? To the tasks of the revolution which we have enumerated it adds nothing whatsoever.[13]

It is, at first sight, a very powerful argument. But what, then, of the defence of the USSR?

The defence of the USSR coincides for us with the preparation of world revolution. Only those methods are permissible which do not conflict with the interests of the revolution. The defence of the USSR is related to the world socialist revolution as a tactical task is related to a strategic one. A tactic is subordinated to a strategic goal and in no case can be in contradiction to the latter.[14]

If, therefore, the requirements of the tactical operation do in fact come into conflict with the strategic aim (as Trotsky's left-wing critics believed it must) then the tactic - defence of the USSR - must be sacrificed. On that basis, it would seem, Trotsky's critics (those who considered themselves revolutionaries, that is) might easily agree to differ with his terminology. Why split over mere words?

In reality, Trotsky believed, much more was at stake. If the bureaucracy really constituted a *class* and the USSR a new form of *exploitative* society, Trotsky argued, then it could not be assumed that Stalinist Russia was the highly exceptional product of unique circumstances, nor could it be assumed that it was soon doomed to disappear, as he was convinced it was.

Nor could matters be left there. Trotsky drew attention to a view that was 'in the air', so to speak, at the end of the thirties; that 'bureaucratisation' and 'statisation' were on the increase everywhere and indicated the shape of society to come - the 'totalitarian statism' which he himself expected to develop unless the proletarian revolution followed the war. Orwell's *1984* (published in 1944) expressed the mood. Thus the question became confused with 'the world historical perspective for the next decades if not centuries: Have we entered the epoch of social revolution and socialist society, or on the contrary the epoch of the declining society of totalitarian bureaucracy?'[15]

The alternatives were falsely put. The predictions of *The Bureaucratisation of the World* (the title of a book by Bruno Rizzi, which Trotsky cited) were impressionistic, not the product of analysis. Nor did it follow that if the USSR were indeed an exploitative society in the marxist sense (and this is what the apparently scholastic arguments of whether the bureaucracy was a 'class' or a 'caste' - Trotsky's term - were really about), that it was a *fundamentally new* type of exploitative society. Suppose it was a form of capitalism? If so, all the arguments about 'world historical perspective' fall to the ground.

Trotsky was, of course, familiar with the concept of state capitalism. In *the Revolution Betrayed* he wrote:

Theoretically, to be sure, it is possible to conceive a situation in which the bourgeoisie as a whole constitutes itself as a stock company which, by means of its state, administers the whole national economy. The economic laws of such a regime would present no mysteries. A single capitalist, as is well known, receives in the form of profit, not that part of the surplus value which is created by the workers of his own enterprise, but a share of the combined surplus value created throughout the country proportionate to the amount of his own capital. Under an integral 'state capitalism', this law of the equal rate of profit would be realised, not by devious routes - that is competition among different capitals - but immediately and directly through state bookkeeping. Such a regime never existed, however, and, because of profound contradictions among the proprietors themselves, will never exist - the more so since, in its quality of universal repository of capitalist property, the state would be too tempting an object of social revolution.[16]

Although, Trotsky thought, a system of 'integral' (that is, total) state capitalism was theoretically possible, it would not come into existence. But suppose a bourgeoisie had been destroyed by a revolution and the proletariat - due to its numerical and cultural weakness - fails to take, or having taken, fails to hold, power. What then? A bureaucracy, emerging as a privileged layer (as Trotsky had graphically described in the case of Stalin's bureaucracy in the USSR) becomes the master of the state and the economy. What, actually, would be its *economic* role? Would it not be a 'substitute' capitalist class? It cannot be argued that it is not capitalist because it controls the entire national economy. Trotsky had conceded that, in principle, a statised bourgeoisie could occupy that position. The only *serious* argument that could be advanced, on Trotsky's analysis, is the one he advanced himself. 'The bureaucracy owns neither stocks nor bonds.' Two points have to be made in this

108

connection: first, the minor point, is that it is simply not true - anyone who can afford it in the USSR can buy various kinds of state bonds which bear interest and can be inherited by heirs on the payment of a modest inheritance tax (*much* lower than the corresponding taxes in the West, just as the top rates of income tax are *much* lower in the USSR than in most Western capitalist countries). Second, the major point, from a marxist point of view, is that the individual capitalist's consumption is, as Marx himself put it, a 'robbery perpetrated on accumulation'; that is, it is a drain on resources that could otherwise have gone towards accumulation, and is certainly not the major consideration. The *major* consideration is who controls the accumulation process.

Returning to the question in 1939 Trotsky wrote:

We have rejected, and still reject, this term [state capitalism] which, while it does correctly characterise certain features of the Soviet state, nevertheless ignores its fundamental difference from capitalist states, namely, the absence of a bourgeoisie as a class of property owners, the existence of the state form of ownership of the most important means of production, and finally planned economy made possible by the October revolution.[17]

Trotsky consistently approached the analysis of Stalinist society from the standpoint of the *form of property*, not the actual social relations of production - although he often used that phrase and, indeed, treated the two as identical. But they are not.

In criticising Proudhon, Marx had explained:

Thus to define bourgeois property is nothing less than to give an exposition of all the social relations of bourgeois production. To try to give a definition of property as of an independent relation, a category apart - an abstract eternal idea - can be nothing but an illusion of metaphysics or jurisprudence.[18]

109

And so with the USSR. The form of property (state ownership in this case) cannot be considered independently of the social relations of production. The *dominant* relation of production in the USSR (especially after industrialisation) was the wage labour/capital relationship characteristic of capitalism - and still is. The worker in the USSR sells a commodity, labour power, in the same way as a worker does in the USA. Nor is he or she paid in rations like a slave, or in a share of the produce like a serf, but in money which is spent on commodities, goods produced for sale.

Wage labour implies capital. There is no bourgeoisie in the USSR. But there is certainly capital - as Marx defined capital. Capital, it need hardly be said, does not, for a marxist, consist of machinery, raw materials, credits and so on. Capital is 'an independent social *power*, i.e., as the power of a part of a society it maintains itself and increases by exchange for *direct living labour power*. The existence of a class which owns nothing but its capacity for labour is a necessary prerequisite of capital. It is only the domination of accumulated, past materialised labour over direct living labour which turns accumulated labour into capital.'[19] Such a state of affairs certainly exists in the USSR.

For Marx, the bourgeoisie's significance was as the 'personification of Capital'. In the USSR the bureaucracy fulfils this function. This last point Trotsky directly denied. For him, the bureaucracy was merely 'a gendarme' in the process of distribution, determining who gets what and when. But this is inseparable from the direction of the process of capital accumulation. The implication that the bureaucracy does not direct the accumulation process, that is, does not act as the 'personification' of capital, will not stand a moment's examination. If not the bureaucracy, then who? Certainly not the working class.

The last point illustrates exactly the *essential* distinction between a genuine transitional society (workers' state, dictatorship of the proletariat) in which wage labour will inevitably persist for some time, and any form of capitalism. Collective working class control over the economy *modifies* (and eventually eliminates) the wage labour/capital relationship. Take that away and, in an industrial society, the power of capital is restored. The concept of a workers' state is meaningless without some degree of workers' control over society.

Of course, if the society of the USSR is described as a form of state capitalism, it must be conceded that it is a highly peculiar capitalist society - although, of course, it is *incomparably* closer to capitalist norms than to a workers' state, distorted or otherwise. A discussion of the peculiarities and dynamics of the USSR is not pertinent here. By far the best analysis will be found in Tony Cliff's *State Capitalism in Russia*.[20] What is relevant is Trotsky's failure to examine the actual relations of production in the USSR and its consequences. His final view was:

> A totalitarian regime, whether of Stalinist or fascist type, by its very essence can be only a temporary transitional regime. Naked dictatorship in history has generally been the product and symptom of an especially severe social crisis, and not at all of a stable regime. Severe crisis cannot be a permanent condition of society. A totalitarian state is capable of suppressing social contradictions during a certain period, but it is incapable of perpetuating itself. The monstrous purges in the USSR are most convincing testimony of the fact that Soviet society organically tends towards ejection of the bureaucracy ... Symptomatic of this oncoming death agony, by the sweep and monstrous fraudulence of his purge, Stalin testifies to nothing else but the incapacity of the bureaucracy to transform itself into a stable ruling class. Might we not place ourselves in a ludicrous position if we affixed to the Bonapartist oligarchy the nomenclature of a new ruling class just a few years or even a few months prior to its inglorious downfall?[21]

That downfall, it will be recalled, was to be expected either because the bureaucracy, 'becoming ever more the organ of the world bourgeoisie...will overthrow the new forms of property', or because of a proletarian revolution (or, of course, foreign conquest). And it was to be expected in the near future - in 'a few years or even a few months'.

This was the assessment Trotsky bequeathed to his followers and, like his perspective for western capitalism, it would disorient them. But the existence of a wing of the bureaucracy wishing to restore capitalism proved to be a myth at least on any relevant time scale. (Trotsky's belief in it was in flagrant contradiction with his own view of the possibility of totalitarian statism in the developed capitalist countries.)

The USSR emerged from the war stronger than before (relative to other powers) with the bureaucracy firmly in the saddle on the basis of nationalised industry. Moreover, it imposed regimes along the lines of the Russian model in Poland, Czechoslovakia, Hungary, Rumania, Bulgaria, East Germany and North Korea. As has been noted, 'indigenous' Stalinist regimes came to power in Albania, Yugoslavia and, a little later, in China and North Vietnam *without* significant direct intervention by the Russian army. Stalinism, evidently, was not in its 'death agony' but was, in the absence of proletarian revolution, an alternative means of capital accumulation to 'classical' state monopoly capitalism.

Deflected Permanent Revolution

The industrial working class played no role whatever in the Chinese Communist Party's conquest of power in 1948-49. Nor did workers play any role *inside* the CCP.

To take the last point first. Whereas, at the end of 1925, workers made up over 66 per cent of the CCP (peasants 5.0 per cent, the rest various urban petty bourgeoisie, amongst whom intellectuals were prominent), by September 1930 the proportion of workers, by the CCP's own data, was down to 1.6 per cent.[22]

Thereafter the figure was effectively zero until after Mao Tse-tung's forces had conquered China.

After the defeat of the 'Canton Commune' at the end of 1927, the remnants of the CCP retreated deep into the country-side and resorted to guerilla warfare. The peasant 'Kiangsi Soviet Republic' was established, with fluctuating territories in central China and, when it was finally overrun by Chiang Kai-shek's forces in 1934, the Red Army undertook the 'long march' to Shensi in the far north-west. This heroic operation, carried out against overwhelming odds, took the party-army (it being increasingly difficult to distinguish them) into an area utterly remote from urban life, modern industry and the Chinese working class. Chu Teh, then the senior military commander, himself admitted, 'The regions under the direction of the Communists are the most backward economically in the whole country . . . '[23] And that country was *China*, then one of the most backward countries in the world.

There, for more than ten years, the CCP forces carried on their struggle for survival against Chiang's armies (although nominally in alliance with Chiang after 1935) and the Japanese invaders. A state machine was constructed in this wholly peasant country on the usual hierarchical and authoritarian lines, consisting of declassed urban intellectuals at the top and peasants at the base. The Japanese army controlled all the areas with significant industrial development from 1937 to 1945, Manchuria (where there was industrial growth) and the coastal cities where industry (and the proletariat) diminished.

With the Japanese surrender in 1945, Kuomintang forces reoccupied most of China with US help, but the utterly corrupt KMT regime was by then in an advanced state of disintegration. After attempts at a national KMT-CCP coalition government had broken down, the CCP conquered its demoralised and fragmenting opponent by purely military means. Massive US military supplies and support to the KMT did not affect the outcome. KMT units, up to divisional and even corps strength, deserted wholesale - often complete with their generals.

Mao's strategy was to encourage these transfers of allegiance and to dampen down *any* independent action by either peasants or workers - but especially the latter. The Communist Party was completely divorced from the working class. Before the fall of Peking Lin Piao, the CCP army commander in the area, and later Mao's heir until his disgrace and death in 1971, issued a proclamation calling on the workers *not* to revolt but to 'maintain order and continue in their present occupations. Kuomintang officials and police personnel of the city, county or other level of government institution . . . are enjoined to remain at their posts.'[24] In January 1949 the KMT general in command of the Peking garrison surrendered. 'Order' was preserved. One military governor took over from another.

It was the same when the CCP forces approached the Yangtse River and the great cities of central China such as Shanghai and Hankow, and which had been the storm centres of revolution in 1925-26. A special proclamation issued under the signatures of Mao Tse-tung (head of government) and Chu Teh (army commander-in-chief) declared that:

> workers and employees in all trades will continue to work and that business will continue as usual . . . officials of the Kuomintang . . . of various levels . . . [and] police personnel are to stay at their posts and obey the orders of the People's Liberation Army and the People's government.[25]

A strange revolution with 'business as usual'! And so it went on to the end, and the proclamation of the 'People's Republic' in October 1949. For these reasons many of Trotsky's followers, including the leaders of the American SWP, denied that any *real* change had taken place for several years after 1949.

This proved to be wrong. A real overturn had occurred. But of what kind? Central to the theory of Permanent Revolution was the belief that the bourgeoisie in backward countries was incapable of leading a bourgeois revolution. That was confirmed, yet again. Equally central was the belief that only the working class could lead the mass of the peasantry and urban petty-bourgeoisie in the democratic revolution which would then fuse with the socialist revolution. That proved false. The Chinese working class, in the absence of any *mass* revolutionary workers' movement elsewhere in the world, remained passive. Nor did the peasantry refute Marx's view of their inability to play an *independent* political role. 1949 was not a peasant movement.

Yet a revolution did occur. China was unified. The imperialist powers were excluded from Chinese soil. The agrarian question, if not 'solved', was at any rate resolved so far as is possible, short of socialism, by the liquidation of land-lordism. All the *essential* features of the bourgeois (or democratic) revolution, as understood by Trotsky himself, had been achieved *except* political freedom in which the workers' movement could develop.

They had been gained under the leadership of declassed intellectuals who, in circumstances of general social breakdown, had built a peasant army and conquered by military means a regime rotten to the point of dissolution. Over 2,000 years earlier, the Han dynasty itself had been founded in similar circumstances, under the leadership of a dynastic founder who, like Mao, came from a rich peasant family. But in the mid-twentieth century, survival for the new regime depended on industrialisation. Chinese Stalinism had its roots in this necessity. It was a development for which Trotsky had failed to allow. In itself, that is neither surprising nor important. But, taken in conjunction with the other unexpected outcomes, it was to have a significant effect on the future of Trotsky's movement.

Only the Chinese case has been considered here - on the grounds of its overwhelming importance - but, earlier, Yugoslavia and Albania and, later, North Vietnam and Cuba, showed certain similar features. The term 'deflected permanent revolution' was introduced by Tony Cliff to describe the phenomenon,[26] so different from the theory of Permanent Revolution as Trotsky understood it.

Trotskyism After Trotsky

The political dilemmas that faced Trotsky's followers in the years after his death are relevant here for two reasons; first, because Trotsky himself believed in the supreme importance of the Fourth International; second, because of the further light they shed on the strengths and weaknesses of his ideas.

Trotsky's uncompromising revolutionary internationalism had steeled his followers to resist an accommodation with the 'democratic' imperialism of the allied camp during the second world war, in spite of enormous pressure (including the pressure of the overwhelming mass of the working class, and most of its best and most militant elements). They had indeed 'swum against the stream' and emerged unbowed, in spite of persecutions, imprisonments (in the USA and Britain, not to mention the Nazi-occupied countries) and executions which eliminated a significant number of Trotskyist activists in Europe.

They had preserved the tradition against all the odds, recruited new members and, in some cases at least, had become more working class in composition (this was certainly true of the Americans and the British). They were inspired and fortified by the vision of proletarian revolution in the near future. Thus, the main British group issued as a pamphlet in 1944, its 1942 perspectives document under the title *Preparing for Power*! There were not more than two to three hundred of them at the time ... This magnificent disregard for immediate and apparently insuperable difficulties combined with an unshaken faith in the future was directly inspired by Trotsky's ideas. It was typical of Trotsky's followers everywhere.

Unfortunately, it had another side: a literal belief in the detailed accuracy of Trotsky's 1938-40 world outlook and predictions. Two distinct elements, revolutionary internationalism with faith in the ultimate triumph of socialism, and *specific*

116

assessments of the prospects for capitalism and Stalinism, had become fused. Consequently, attention to the realities of a fast-changing situation became, in the eyes of the more 'orthodox' of Trotsky's followers, akin to 'revisionism'. For several years after 1945 the movement was stuck, in its majority, in the '1938 groove'.

When it eventually broke out, a number of different currents emerged, some preserving rather more elements of the authentic communist tradition, others a good many less. Their greatest weakness was their inability for the most part to resist fully the gravitational pull of Stalinism and, a little later, in the fifties and sixties, Third Worldism. This, in turn, led them away from sustained and single-minded concentration on recreating a revolutionary current in the industrial working class. So their predominantly petty-bourgeois character was reinforced, and a vicious circle was perpetuated.

All that said, it remains true that the heritage of Trotsky's lifelong struggle, the last years of which were carried on under conditions of incredible difficulty, is immensely valuable. To all those marxists for whom marxism is a synthesis of theory and *practice*, and not merely more or less learned commentary, it is an indispensable contribution to that synthesis today.

References

Introduction / pp.1-6
1. P. Anderson, *Considerations on Western Marxism*, London: New Left Books 1976, p.29.

1. Permanent Revolution / pp.7-26
1. Engels to Kautsky, *Marx and Engels: Selected Correspondence 1846-1895*, London: Lawrence & Wishart 1936, p.399.
2. 'Manifesto of the Russian Social-Democratic Workers' Party', (1898), in R.V. Daniels (ed.), *A Documentary History of Communism*, New York: Vintage 1962, Vol.1, p.7.
3. Lenin, *Collected Works*, Moscow: Foreign Languages Publishing House 1960, Vol.9, pp.55-57. Emphasis in original.
4. *Ibid.* Vol.21, p.33.
5. Trotsky, 'Our differences', in *1905*, New York: Vintage 1972, p.312.
6. *Ibid.*
7. *Ibid.* pp.313-14.
8. Trotsky, 'Results and prospects', in *The Permanent Revolution*, 1962, pp.194-95. Emphasis added.
9. Lenin, *Collected Works*, *op.cit.* Vol.9, p.28.
10. Trotsky, 'Our differences', *op.cit.* p.317.
11. It would take us too far afield from the limited purpose of this book to attempt to justify these statements. Trotsky's own *History of the Russian Revolution*, London: Sphere 1977, and Pluto Press 1978, Vols. I and II; and Tony Cliff's *Lenin*, London: Pluto Press 1976, Vol.2, provide, from slightly different angles, the decisive evidence.
12. T. Cliff, *Lenin*, London: Pluto Press 1976, Vol.2, p.138.
13. I. Deutscher, *The Prophet Unarmed*, London: Oxford University Press 1959, p.323.
14. Trotsky, 'The Chinese Communist Party and the Kuomintang', *Leon Trotsky on China*, New York: Monad 1976, pp.113-15.
15. Trotsky, 'First speech on the Chinese question', *Leon Trotsky on China*, *op.cit.* p.227.
16. Trotsky, 'Summary and perspectives of the Chinese revolution', *Leon Trotsky on China*, *op.cit.* p.297.
17. Trotsky, 'The Chinese revolution and the theses of Comrade Stalin', *Leon Trotsky on China*, *op.cit.* pp.162-63.

2. Stalinism / pp.27-47
1. Lenin, *Collected Works*, Moscow: Foreign Languages Publishing House 1960, Vol.33, pp.65-66.
2. E.H. Carr, *The Bolshevik Revolution*, Harmondsworth: Penguin 1963, Vol.2, pp.194-200.

3. V. Serge, *From Lenin to Stalin*, New York: Monad 1973, p.39.
4. Trotsky, in I. Deutscher, *The Prophet Armed*, London: Oxford University Press 1954, p.509.
5. Lenin, *op.cit.* Vol.32, p.24.
6. *Ibid.* p.48.
7. A detailed account is given in I. Deutscher, *The Prophet Unarmed*, London: Oxford University Press 1959, especially chapters 2 and 5.
8. *Platform of the Opposition*, London: New Park 1973, pp.35-36.
9. Stalin, in Trotsky, *The Revolution Betrayed*, London: New Park 1967, p.291.
10. Trotsky, 'Where is the Soviet Republic going?', *Writings of Leon Trotsky 1929*, New York: Pathfinder Press 1975, pp.47-48.
11. *Ibid.* p.50.
12. *Ibid.* p.51.
13. Trotsky, 'Problems of the development of the USSR', *Writings of Leon Trotsky 1930-31*, New York: Pathfinder Press 1973, p.215.
14. *Ibid.* p.225. Emphasis in original.
15. A. Nove, *An Economic History of the USSR*, Harmondsworth: Penguin 1965, p.206.
16. Trotsky, 'The class nature of the Soviet State', *Writings of Leon Trotsky 1933-34*, New York: Pathfinder Press 1972, pp.117-18. Emphasis in original.
17. Trotsky, 'The workers' state, Thermidor and Bonapartism', *Writings of Leon Trotsky 1934-35*, New York: Pathfinder Press 1971, pp.166-67.
18. *Ibid.* p.182.
19. I. Deutscher, *op.cit.* p.139.
20. Trotsky, 'The workers' state, Thermidor and Bonapartism', *op.cit.* pp.172-73. Emphasis in original.
21. Trotsky, 'The death agony of capitalism and the tasks of the Fourth International', *Documents of the Fourth International*, New York: Pathfinder Press 1973, p.210. Emphasis in original.
22. *Ibid.* p.211.
23. *Ibid.* p.211-12.
24. Trotsky, *The Revolution Betrayed*, London: New Park 1967, p.278.
25. Trotsky, 'The death agony . . . ', *op.cit.* p.213. Emphasis in original.
26. Trotsky, *The Revolution Betrayed*, *op.cit.* p.254.
27. *Ibid.* p.255.

3. Strategy and Tactics / pp.48-75

1. Trotsky, 'Manifesto of the Communist International to the workers of the world', *The First Five Years of the Communist International*, New York: Pioneer 1945, Vol.1, pp.29-30.
2. J. Degras, *The Communist International 1919-43*, London: Cass 1971, Vol.I, p.16.
3. *Ibid.* p.6.
4. Lenin, *Collected Works*, Moscow: Foreign Languages Publishing House 1960, Vol.28, p.455.

5. S. Haffner, *Failure of a Revolution: Germany 1918-19*, London: Andre Deutsch 1973, p.152.
6. Lenin, *op.cit*. Vol.21, p.40.
7. J. Degras, *op.cit*. Vol.1, pp.12-13.
8. J. Degras, *op.cit*. p.19.
9. Lenin, *op.cit*. Vol.25, p.393.
10. *Ibid*. Vol.29, p.311.
11. J. Degras, *op.cit*. p.13.
12. Lenin, *op.cit*. Vol.31, pp.206-07.
13. *Ibid*. p.206.
14. J. Degras, *op.cit*. p.109.
15. Trotsky, 'Speech on Comrade Zinoviev's report on the role of the party', *The First Five Years of the Communist International*, *op.cit*. Vol.1, pp.97-99.
16. *Ibid*. p.101.
17. *Ibid*. p.141.
18. *Ibid*. pp.303-05.
19. *Ibid*. pp.294-95.
20. J. Degras, *op.cit*. Vol.I, p.230.
21. Trotsky, *The First Five Years of the Communist International*, *op.cit*. Vol.2, pp.91-95.
22. Trotsky, *Writings of Leon Trotsky 1932-33*, New York: Pathfinder Press 1972, pp.51-55.
23. E.H. Carr, *The Interregnum 1923-1924*, Harmondsworth: Penguin 1965, p.221.
24. Trotsky, 'Lessons of the General Strike', *Trotsky's Writings on Britain*, London: New Park 1974, Vol.II, pp.241, 245.
25. *Ibid*. p.244. Emphasis in original.
26. *Ibid*. pp.252-53.
27. J. Degras, *The Communist International: Documents*, London: Cass, Vol.III, p.44.
28. *Ibid*. p.159.
29. *Ibid*. p.224.
30. Trotsky, 'The turn in the Communist International', *The Struggle Against Fascism in Germany*, New York: Pathfinder Press 1971, pp.57-60. Emphasis in original.
31. Trotsky, 'What next?', *The Struggle Against Fascism in Germany*, *op.cit*. p.248.
32. *Ibid*. p.254.
33. J. Degras, *op.cit*. Vol.III, p.375.
34. *Ibid*. p.390.
35. *Ibid*. p.384.
36. See F. Morrow, *Revolution and Counter-Revolution in Spain*, New York: Pioneer 1938, p.34.
37. *Ibid*. p.35.
38. Trotsky, 'The lessons of Spain: the last warning', *The Spanish Revolution (1931-39)*, New York: Pathfinder Press 1973, pp.322-23.

4. Party and Class / pp.76-95

1. I. Deutscher, *The Prophet Armed*, London: Oxford University Press 1954, p.45.

2. *1903: Second Congress of the Russian Social-Democratic Labour Party*, London: New Park, p.204.

3. Trotsky, 'Our political tasks', in R.V. Daniels (ed.), *A Documentary History of Communism*, New York: Vintage 1962, Vol.1, p.31.

4. See Schurer, 'The Permanent Revolution', in Labedz (ed.), *Revisionism*, London: Allen & Unwin 1962, p.73. Emphasis added.

5. *Ibid.* p.74.

6. See T. Cliff, *Lenin*, London: Pluto Press 1976, Vol.1, pp.168-179, Vol.2, pp.97-139.

7. Trotsky, 'What next?', *The Struggle Against Fascism in Germany*, New York: Pathfinder Press 1971, p.163. Emphasis in original.

8. *Ibid.* pp.163-64.

9. *Ibid.* p.159.

10. Trotsky, 'Manifesto of the Communist International to the workers of the world', *The First Five Years of the Communist International*, New York: Pioneer 1945, Vol.1, p.29.

11. Trotsky, 'What next?', *op.cit.* p.254.

12. Trotsky, 'The Spanish revolution and the danger threatening it', *The Spanish Revolution (1931-39)*, New York: Pathfinder Press 1973, p.133.

13. Trotsky, 'The groupings in the communist opposition', *Writings of Leon Trotsky 1929*, New York: Pathfinder Press 1975, p.81.

14. Trotsky, 'The international left opposition: its tasks and methods', *Writings of Leon Trotsky 1932-33*, New York: Pathfinder Press 1972, p.56.

15. Trotsky, *History of the Russian Revolution*, London: Sphere 1977, Vol.1, p.306.

16. Trotsky, 'The evolution of the Comintern', *Documents of the Fourth International*, New York: Pathfinder Press 1973, Vol.1, p.128.

17. Trotsky, 'Thermidor and Bonapartism', *Writings of Leon Trotsky 1930-31*, New York: Pathfinder Press 1973, p.75.

18. Trotsky, 'For a workers' united front against fascism', *The Struggle Against Fascism in Germany*, *op.cit.* p.134. Emphasis in original.

19. Trotsky, 'Germany: key to the international situation', *The Struggle Against Fascism in Germany*, *op.cit.* pp.121-22.

20. Trotsky, 'The Stalin bureaucracy in straits', *Writings of Leon Trotsky 1932*, New York: Pathfinder Press 1973, p.125.

21. Trotsky, 'To the editorial board of *Prometeo*', *Writings of Leon Trotsky 1930*, New York: Pathfinder Press 1975, pp.285-286.

22. T. Cliff, *Lenin*, London: Pluto Press 1976, Vol.2, p.12.

23. J. van Heijenoort, *With Trotsky in Exile*, Boston: Harvard University Press 1978, p.38.

24. Trotsky, 'Lessons of the SFIO entry', *Writings of Leon Trotsky 1935-36*, New York: Pathfinder Press 1970, p.31.

25. Trotsky, 'It is time to stop', *Writings of Leon Trotsky 1933-34*, New York: Pathfinder Press 1972, pp.90-91.

26. Trotsky, 'Centrist alchemy or marxism', *Writings of Leon Trotsky 1934-35*, New York: Pathfinder Press 1971, p.274.

27. Trotsky, 'A great achievement', *Writings of Leon Trotsky 1937-38*, New York: Pathfinder Press 1976, p.439.

5. The Heritage / 96-117

1. See *The Moscow Trials: An Anthology*, London: New Park 1967, p.12.

2. See I. Deutscher, *The Prophet Outcast*, New York: Vintage 1964, p.171.

3. Trotsky, 'Fighting against the stream', *Writings of Leon Trotsky 1938-39*, New York: Pathfinder Press 1974, p.251-52.

4. Trotsky, 'The death agony of capitalism and the tasks of the Fourth International', *Documents of the Fourth International*, New York: Pathfinder Press 1973, p.180.

5. Trotsky, 'The USSR in war', *In Defence of Marxism*, London: New Park 1971, p.9.

6. Trotsky, 'The death agony . . .', *op.cit.* p.183.

7. *Ibid.* p.182.

8. Trotsky, 'The Comintern's liquidation congress', *Writings of Leon Trotsky 1935-36*, New York: Pathfinder Press 1970, p.11.

9. Trotsky, 'The USSR in war', *op.cit.* p.10.

10. M. Kidron, *Western Capitalism Since the War*, Harmondsworth: Penguin 1967, p.11.

11. Trotsky, 'The founding of the Fourth International', *Writings of Leon Trotsky 1938-39*, *op.cit.* p.87.

12. Trotsky, 'The death agony . . .', *op.cit.* p.183.

13. Trotsky, 'The USSR in war', *op.cit.* pp.4-5.

14. *Ibid.* p.21.

15. *Ibid.* p.18.

16. Trotsky, *The Revolution Betrayed*, London: New Park 1967, pp.245-46.

17. Trotsky, 'Ten years', *Writings of Leon Trotsky 1938-39*, *op.cit.* p.341.

18. Marx, *Poverty of Philosophy*, London: Lawrence & Wishart 1937, pp.129-30.

19. Marx, 'Wage labour and capital', *Selected Works of Marx and Engels*, London: Lawrence & Wishart 1934, pp.265-66.

20. T. Cliff, *State Capitalism in Russia*, London: Pluto Press 1974, p.276.

21. Trotsky, 'The USSR in war', *op.cit.* pp.16-17.

22. Isaacs, *The Tragedy of the Chinese Revolution*, London: Secker & Warburg 1938, p.394.

23. See T. Cliff, 'Permanent Revolution', *International Socialism*, 1962, No.12, p.17.

24. *Ibid.* p.18.

25. *Ibid.*

26. *Ibid.*